Stepping Out of Otherness

What might the impact be on a grown woman of having a nursery school teacher change and anglicise her name at the age of three? That three-year-old was me. In our world, we face more and more polarisation and so it feels imperative that we understand the concept and lived experience of "Othering". Othering takes away individuality and reduces whole groups to "they".

This book explores the theory, examining why Othering is so much part of human biology and conditioning. Through a narrative approach, the experiences of women of colour growing up in 1970s and 1980s Britain are explored, sharing individual stories and common themes. Ultimately this book is a celebration of their deep commitment to self-work and development and their success in navigating the additional burden of being different.

We hear from other thinkers and activists, and offer active hope and potential ways forward in how we might create more inclusive, sustainable societies. This is a monumental task but arguably we have no choice, and so the work of changing how we choose to live feels like the most important work we can do together.

Rita Symons is a second-generation British Asian woman. She spent much of her early working life in the NHS, eventually becoming a CEO. She is currently a coach, coach supervisor and facilitator and is the ex-President of a large, professional body for coaching (EMCC UK). She is involved in various groups considering the role of coaching in systemic change and social justice, and considers herself a world citizen.

Stepping Out of Otherness

Women of Colour Finding Their Inner Goddess

Rita Symons

Routledge
Taylor & Francis Group

LONDON AND NEW YORK

Designed cover image: Emily Serena Symons

First published 2025
by Routledge
4 Park Square, Milton Park, Abingdon, Oxon OX14 4RN

and by Routledge
605 Third Avenue, New York, NY 10158

Routledge is an imprint of the Taylor & Francis Group, an informa business

British Library Cataloguing-in-Publication Data
A catalogue record for this book is available from the British Library

ISBN: 978-1-032-48752-6 (hbk)
ISBN: 978-1-032-48750-2 (pbk)
ISBN: 978-1-003-39060-2 (ebk)

DOI: 10.4324/9781003390602

Typeset in Adobe Garamond
by codeMantra

Contents

Contributors

Chapter 4 of this book has been written by the following contributors.

Uma Krishnamoorthy is a Consultant Gynaecologist, Deputy Medical Director and she works to promote a focus on belonging in healthcare.

Jessica Lazarczyk is a mother of two small children, one of whom has been diagnosed with Autism. She is a leadership development coach and organisational psychoanalyst, and is passionate about creating inclusive environments in which all people can thrive.

Andreas Loewe is the Dean of Melbourne, and leads the ministry and mission of St Paul's Anglican Cathedral Melbourne. He chairs the Melbourne Anglican Reconciliation Working Group and is a Senior Fellow at the Faculty of Fine Arts and Music, The University of Melbourne.

Uncle Glenn Loughrey is a Wiradjuri man from New South Wales, and a First Nations Canon of St Paul's Anglican Cathedral Melbourne. An artist who fuses Indigenous arts styles with Western forms of storytelling, he is Associate Professor at the Australian National University.

Janet Mrenica is the founder of the social enterprise Taproot.jem.Systems which has a focus on intersectionality, anti-racism and social justice. She is passionate about sustainability and the climate.

Colleen Qvist is a South African coach and confidential sounding board for healthcare professionals.

Lily Seto is a grandmother, mother, wife, coach, coaching supervisor and practices the art of being a good ancestor. She feels privileged to live, work and play on the traditional lands of the WSÁNEĆ and Coast Salish Peoples, in Western British Columbia, Canada. www.lilyseto.com

Salma Shah is an author, speaker and founder of the award-winning Mastering Your Power programme.

Jennie Tsekwa is a coach, researcher, writer and DE&I Facilitator, based in Johannesburg. She is the founder of the Kopanya Institute which has a focus on inclusion and social justice.

Andréa Watts founded UnglueYou® in 2012 and was the first specialist in coaching with collage. She is a successful speaker and author.

Preface

As a child of Indian Hindu parents growing up in a place where there was little diversity, I was mystified by the religious rituals and multitude of gods and took little interest in the ancient wisdom which was so contrary to what I was taught and the narrative I came to believe. I was brought up in the Global North where a neo-liberalist, largely Christian paradigm prevailed. In my early years, we said the Lord's Prayer at Assembly every morning, being vegetarian was inconceivable as there was only one choice of school dinners and success was defined by owning a nice house, car or possessions.

Only after the death of my mother have I developed a true curiosity about the world's oldest religion and the relevance it may still have in our times. As I have explored Hinduism more, I can be more accepting of the confusing array of gods and see that, ultimately, the religion is about a single universal energy.

I am drawn to the goddess Kali: fierce and powerful, she is seen as both defender of the good in the world and potential destroyer. Devotees talk of the chant or Kali mantra having powerful frequencies which can be transformational and make the seemingly impossible possible. And as I write this, I cannot help but notice that the circle of energy I am taken to is strong *female* energy. I do not, in any way, deny the role of men in societal change, but my assertion is, it is time for women to have a greater voice.

As humanity sits on a precipice of societal, climate and economic breakdown, largely of our own making, the idea that we can draw on a universal, collective energy and learn to live differently feels very appealing. And what if, in that different paradigm, we could learn to override our complex but flawed, error-prone unconscious brain and elevate our consciousness to truly appreciate the unique value of each and every person? I am attracted to the idea of *generative conversations*; those conversations that not only share knowledge, but that create new knowledge. The tool is not complex or technologically advanced: it is human dialogue and connection. Holding onto this feels all the more important with the ever-advancing use of artificial intelligence.

In this book, I explore and invite others to share their wisdom on how we can be more connected at an individual and, therefore, at a societal level.

My ambition is that, through this deepening inter-connection, we could also come to see that, as individuals, we are enough. We have enough; an abundance in contrast to a scarcity mindset. Imagine that world!

My hope for my daughters is that they are able to live in such a world. And this is my hope for humanity as a whole.

Acknowledgements

There are so many people to thank, but I start with the eight women I interviewed for this book. Thank you for stepping into the unknown and potential discomfort to allow the writing of *Stepping Out of Otherness*. Without the richness of your stories and experiences, the theory and hypothecated solutions in this book would be much reduced in impact. I also want to thank the contributors to "Essays on Hope" from across the world. Your different perspectives and wisdom are so truly appreciated and make this much more of a global book, as I am conscious all my research subjects were UK based. You also bring in elements of Othering around difference that go beyond race.

Thank you to those who have given me the opportunity to undertake deep work with truly inspirational colleagues. My work gives me the opportunity to meet so many amazing people, meaning it is thankfully hard to lose hope altogether.

I want to thank dear friends Eve Turner, Colleen Qvist and Lise Lewis for their guidance, review and encouragement, often offered during "Friday Cocktails", a lockdown-initiated activity which we have kept going. If, halfway through, I had not been told this was important work, I may well have given up.

Thanks go to colleagues at Routledge for their support and believing this book was of value in the world.

Particular thanks to Jayna Shepherd, my reviewer, who painstakingly corrected all my errors whilst managing morning sickness, and Dina Desai who took over when my tardiness led to Jayna's baby arriving before my book.

And finally, to my family: my husband and two amazing daughters, who despite their initial bemusement, gave me space and encouragement, and had faith that I have got this.

Introduction

When I said I was writing a book about "Othering", I got a few blank looks. Despite being an important biological and anthropological phenomenon, the concept of and reflection on the subject remains in the shadows and the margins of our consciousness. It is hard to define, as, at one level we are all Other, and indeed we are all responsible for Othering.

I will explore the neuroscience and psychology behind Othering and the evolutionary advantages it has undoubtedly bestowed on humanity. In the complex, fragmented yet interconnected world we now live in, is our natural tendency to "Other" still an advantage or a potential threat to our very existence? The ultimate expression of Othering is dehumanisation, and we have seen all too often the heart-breaking consequences of where this can lead. Can we as a species rise above our biological and social programming and the limited options we believe are our only choices to find a different way to live? I am not alone in my strong desire and hope for this. It is easy to feel hopeless, but I remind myself and connect where I can with the community of individuals across the globe who share a similar outlook. Kashtan (2014) in her beautifully crafted book *Reweaving Our Human Fabric* states that none of us know how, but "The stakes are simply too high to wait for the perfect enough answer, the wise enough leader, or anything else that keeps us from speaking fully what is in our hearts and minds."

So, I hesitantly offer this book as a means to inch forward our understanding of Othering, its impact and how we can make changes in our consciousness and subsequent behaviour. In the words of Jill Bolte Taylor (2021) who, following a stroke, wrote inspirationally: "I love a book that makes me think. But more importantly, I love a book that helps me become more conscious and evolve into my best self." I celebrate this quote as it perfectly captures the spirit of continuous growth and learning.

I also offer an apology if any language or content offends, as I am aware of the sensitivity and individual preferences around terminology. I write this book with an open heart, but recognise this may come with some clumsiness and clunkiness.

DOI: 10.4324/9781003390602-1

The experience of being Othered has a profound impact. One such impact is that on women of colour growing up in the UK in the 1960s, '70s and early '80s. In this book, I tell the stories of eight inspirational women, interwoven with my own experiences, and describe the real-life events, the consequences in early life and the ultimate growth which is characteristic of women who learn very early on that they are different.

This book is about increasing understanding of Othering, but also it is a celebration of the power, resilience and beauty of the women whose stories I feel privileged to share. And in using the gift of their stories, I am not in any way intending to homogenise them, rather, draw common strands from their wonderful uniqueness. The intention in writing this book is to take the power of the story of self and, through thematic analysis, gain new insights into the shared, parallel or contrasting experience of women of colour.

I then share some thoughts on what we can do to collectively move forward, and reflect on the complexity of working in this space, where human minds and hearts are the currency.

Moreover, in the closing "Essays of Hope", I invite a range of thinkers and activists in this area to share their thoughts on what we can do to connect more deeply and surely as individuals and communities, thereby reducing the negative impact of Othering. While sacred rage is understandable and legitimate when we consider the inequalities in the world, I retain a belief that most people are fundamentally good, and so the focus is on what we can do as individuals and communities to connect across the divides. I do not mean to negate the impact of other narratives around injustice, but in offering this book, my intention is to suggest steps forward.

What Do We Mean by "Other"?

In attempting to define Other, we are all unique individuals and so, at some point, we can all be the Other. We forge our identity through a complex process of imposed characteristics or commonly held truths and a continuing process of self-determination. We seek to belong, and we make intentional choices about which people and organisations we affiliate ourselves with. Identity is complex, however, and as we grow, we change and adapt our self-image and how we identify ourselves. The way we now view gender as more fluid, rather than the historic binary definition, is a good example of how societal norms on identify shift over time.

Othering as a concept is related to the deeply human wish to be in a group and is an active process, whereby we exclude individuals or groups in society. It is thought the phrase "Othering" was first coined as a theoretical term in 1985 by Spivak in the context of an exploration of post-colonialisation.

For the purposes of this book, I have adopted a definition by Brons (2015):

> Othering is the simultaneous construction of the self or in-group and
> the other or out-group in mutual and unequal opposition through

identification of some desirable characteristic that the self/in-group has and the Other/out-group lacks and/or some undesirable characteristic that the Other/out-group has and the self/in-group lacks.

Several things strike me about this elegant, inelegant definition. The first is the dichotomy of this being about self and group. Thinking about who and why we Other is potentially a powerful tool for exploration of self, as well as society. The second thing that stands out is the word *unequal*. Othering is about inequality; it is about the exercise of power. The nature of Othering is the belief that the group you belong to is somehow superior. This is often unconscious, but it is real and reverberates in a multitude of ways.

Structure of the Book

The book is divided into five parts or chapters.

Chapter 1 explores evidence and draws on the literature to explore the biological and social causes and manifestations of Othering.

Chapter 2 is based on thematic analysis of interviews with eight unique women of colour who have grown up and gone on to be successful in their chosen fields, in the UK. This explores their lived experience of being "different" together with my own experiences, and shares how they have, through a process of active and continuous reflection, come to a sense of pride and ease in their identity.

Chapter 3 draws on evidence and experience to suggest models which may be useful in our work on inclusion and belonging. My strong desire in this book is not only to raise awareness, but also to offer ways forward in terms of what we can individually and collectively do to reduce Othering.

Chapter 4 brings in the work of collaborators to widen the contribution on our thinking about Othering and leave you, the reader, with some provocations and thoughts about what you might want to commit to, both personally and professionally. In this section, colleagues with different lenses offer readers "Essays on Hope", a collective call to positivity and action.

Chapter 5 offers a brief conclusion which ends the book.

I accept and celebrate that each individual is unique and I also recognise intersectionality and the fact our social identities around race, class, gender and sexuality do indeed intersect and are interwoven in complex ways that may relate to discrimination. For the purposes of this book, however, when I reflect on Othering, it is primarily through the lens of race.

Stop the Othering

Stop Othering people who don't think like you.
Stop Othering people who make different choices than you.
Othering is dismissal. Othering is dehumanizing.

Othering has always led to tragedy. To alienation. To separation.
Whatever the future holds for all of us – division is not the answer. Love is.
Don't let Othering into your heart.
Don't let Othering into your mind.
Stay soft.
Stay open.
Stay kind.
Stay curious.
Stay tolerant.
Stay human.
There are not two "humanities". There is one humanity.
Don't let Othering split us.
We belong together. We belong to each Other.
At our core we are love.
Keep your faith in us.
I know I will.

(Reproduced with the kind permission of Elena Herdieckerhoff)

References

Bolte Taylor, J. (2021) *Whole Brain Living, The Anatomy of Choice and the Four Characteristics that Drive our Life*. London: Hay House UK, p. 259.

Brons, Lajos L. (2015) Othering, an Analysis. *Transcience, a Journal of Global Studies*, 6(1): 69–90.

Herdieckerhoff, E. (2022) Stop the Othering. www.elenaherdieckerhoff.com/new-blog/a-poem-about-othering (Accessed 22 February 2023).

Kashtan, M. (2014) *Reweaving the Human Fabric: Working Together to Create a Nonviolent Future*. Oakland, CA: Fearless Heart Publication.

1

Why Are We So Good at Othering?

Reality as a Social Construct

Ada Palmer (2017) shares: "It doesn't take a declaration, or an invasion, to start a war, all it takes is an 'us' and a 'them'. And a spark."

Othering is a very real phenomenon, which lies at the centre of much of the social inequity we see around us. It is consistent with Luckman and Berger's (1966) theory of social constructionism, which argues that there is no such thing as a single true reality and reality in fact is created or constructed by people, with different perspectives, sense making in order to build a coherent truth.

The concept of truth is, therefore, inevitably subjective rather than normative. How we direct our consciousness to interpret what we observe is also then subjective. So, what factors influence how we draw meaning from the world around us and the behaviours we observe? A difficult question to answer, as we consider the complex interaction of nature and nurture.

What then does this mean in respect to how people perceive difference? Again, if we believe in social constructionism, our beliefs about gender, race, sexuality and all the other dimensions we use to put people in boxes are also social constructs. We only have to look at how society's attitudes have changed through generations to intrinsically know this.

Weick (1995) states: "People make sense of things by seeing a world on which they already imposed what they believe. In other words, people discover their own inventions. This is why *sensemaking* can be understood as invention and interpretations understood as discovery."

The problem I have with social constructionism is the implication that reality only exists in so far as we, that is, humanity, create it through social interaction.

DOI: 10.4324/9781003390602-2

This plays into the dominant neo-liberalist ideology that we are somehow separate from nature and the world is here for us to use and plunder.

Onuf (1989) develops the theory further and introduces the phrase "social constructivism". This sits more comfortably as a theory as it recognises social activity and human connection as one way of creating meaning, but we also gain meaning from objects, other sentient beings, and the other elements of the earth. It may feel like semantics, but I will adopt the framework of social constructivism in this exploration, recognising the dualism of the power of human interaction, while acknowledging our paths are interwoven with all other living things. It feels important to connect our aspirations around racial and social harmony and equity with our need to consider ourselves part of nature, not master of it. One requisite for us to evolve in a sustainable way is, I would suggest, a move from anthropocentric approaches which place humans at the centre to a position where we see ourselves as part of nature.

If we acknowledge that our realities are socially constructed, then we can only build our reality with the set of bricks or pieces we have access to. This is based on our life experience, our family and community, our schooling, our geographical location and the events which have shaped us.

How then can we become more curious about other people's building blocks? And to what extent are the life experiences of minoritised groups littered with negative experiences, based on the assumptions others make, which shape and limit their aspirations of what they can build?

One can conclude that if our reality is socially constructed, we need to consider the notion of race as a moveable and social phenomenon, not a biological truth. The concept of race constructivism emerges.

Our categorisation and hierarchical approach to race can arguably be traced back to world trade and colonialism. In Elizabethan times, powerful merchants appealed to Queen Elizabeth I to allow them to sail to the Indian Ocean. In 1591, James Lancaster led the first successful British landing in India, sailing on the *Bonaventure*, conveniently looting Spanish and Portuguese ships on the way. Large, powerful businesses such as the East India Company were created. The narrative of "savages" and the subsequent devaluing of those whose ancestors had inhabited those lands allowed large companies, not nation states, to seize large parts of the southern hemisphere. This led the way for colonialism and the dehumanising of large proportions of the world's population in order to generate more wealth. The slave trade was a tragic but almost inevitable consequence of this. Race is very much a social construct and one that was specifically designed to support the accumulation of mass wealth by a minority.

I have only myself become aware of some of this history in my early fifties. I am more involved in work around inclusion and, as part of a programme for a large, socially focussed corporation, I am delivering sessions on the history of racism. The participants' most common reaction is one of shock, sadness and shame. And I too, in a parallel process, feel shame. How could I have grown into my fifties before knowing this truth? The answer: because I was never taught it.

James and Burgos (2022) conclude:

> Normatively, race constructivists argue that since society labels people according to racial categories, and since such labelling often leads to race-based differences in resources, opportunities, and well-being, the concept of race must be conserved, in order to facilitate race-based social movements or policies, such as affirmative action, that compensate for socially constructed but socially relevant racial differences.

From this we can conclude we have historically created inequity, and so to deny race as a concept is not helpful. Rather, we need to accept the inequality our forebearers have established and actively seek to redress the balance.

Powell (2018) states in a joint paper on Othering: "I think to be Othered is to be denied the fullness of one's humanity. Othering, therefore, appears to violate a fairly basic human right, making parts of our communities invisible." So again, the concept that we have conveniently denigrated large parts of society requires, I would suggest, an active, not a passive, response.

In addressing our challenges, I believe change truly does happen one conversation at a time and relationships and emotional capital are our greatest tools. If reality is ours to shape, we can and should remain hopeful that we have the ability to create a positive shift if we prioritise meaningful human connection. And that may then make those invisible communities more solid and substantial and help us to create more equitable societies.

There are clearly global issues at play, but I was reminded by a colleague of the African Proverb: "if you think you are too small to make a difference, try sleeping in a tent with a mosquito". So, maybe the place to start is with small individual steps.

Our Need to Belong

A basic cognitive process which is critical to understanding Othering is identified through social identity theory. Tajfel et al. (1979) conceived this as the suggestion that, as humans, we create our identity, and subsequently our self-esteem, by identifying with groups. The need to belong is strong and real, but it can have negative consequences. They identify three distinct phases by which we create social identity, and, through this process, we often inadvertently accentuate inequality.

1. *Social Categorisation*: We literally put people into boxes, albeit people can be in multiple boxes. We categorise people in the same way we would group objects to try and make it easier for us to understand the world. Characteristics such as age, colour and gender are easy for us to perceive and so we often use these as the vehicle by which we undertake our crude categorisation.

2. *Social Identification*: So, the next stage is we decide which group or groups we are in and adopt the behaviours of that group. Individuals slowly but surely take on the behaviours they perceive are consistent with that group and this becomes entwined with self-esteem. Good examples of this can be found everywhere, including in the world of cinema. In the 1965 film *The Sound of Music* who can forget the anguished face of Rolf as he battles his affection for the Von Trapp family, Liesl in particular, with his desperation to belong to the Nazi Youth.

3. *Social Comparison*: Having decided on our group, the final stage of social identity theory is to compare our group to Other groups. If we are to feel good emotionally, we do what we can to maintain high self-esteem. We do this by convincing ourselves that our group is better than Other groups. We even use more positive, activist language about our in-group. This results in a spiral where, in order to maintain a feeling of self-worth, those in Other groups are viewed and talked of negatively. We have to believe they are inferior in order to boost and protect our self-image. It is so much easier to externalise than to do the self-work we need to genuinely improve our own self.

Our human need to belong feels positive in some respects, in that connection leads us to feel good. We are, as we have explored, evolved to be social animals. The downside is this often leads to the phenomenon of in-groups and out-groups and this, in turn, forms the basis of most discrimination. By allocating a person to the out-group, we degrade individuals into "they".

In-Group vs Out-group

Assche et al. (2020) demonstrated the challenges of being in the out-group very topically at that time by examining attitudes to social distancing behaviour in the 2020 Covid-19 pandemic. They recruited participants and randomly allocated them to scenarios, exploring their attitudes to behaviours that were not in line with the current rules, for example on social distancing. They found that attitudes to rule breaking or "norm-deviating" behaviour were viewed differently depending on whether individuals were perceived to be in the in- or out-group. Infringement of the rules for out-groups led to more study participants favouring a punitive government response, rather than a collegiate, self-governing response. They demonstrated the tendency we have to trust in those in our group and inherently distrust the out-group. One of their observations was that "negative moral emotions are generalized to the outgroup as a whole".

So, this supports what we know, based on social identity constructs and Othering. We attribute negative characteristics and respond with less humanity to those we perceive to be in the out-group. Interestingly in this study, they also found participants were less likely to advocate supportive measures for the out-group.

Other studies have shown that we have a tendency to homogenise out-groups and treat those in our in-group as unique. In other words, we treat those in our in-group as individuals and those in our out-group as an anonymous "they". In terms of positive regard, we are more generous in our interpretation of behaviour. If someone in your in-group is late, we might be understanding – they have a deadline at work, their child is sick and so on – whereas if someone in the out-group is late the tendency is to revert to they (i.e. everyone we perceive to be in that group) are always late. We, therefore, see our group homogeneity bias in action, supported by a plethora of complementary biases our wonderfully complicated, irrational brains use to simplify the world. One such bias is confirmation bias; we tend to seek out or believe the information which supports what we already believe. This is exacerbated in current times where social media algorithms reinforce and push us to information which strengthens rather than challenges our current belief system.

I personally have ceased reading the comments section of many mainstream newspapers as I find the level of animosity displayed so openly often plunges me into despair. I think for many of us we have had to find strategies to maintain wellbeing which often include active avoidance or limiting exposure to certain media.

Our desire to be in the in-group is perhaps described most poetically by C. S. Lewis in a 1944 Memorial lecture, introducing the concept of "the Lure of the Inner Ring".

He describes the lure of wanting to be in the "inner ring" while posing the juxtaposition that being in the inner circle is not a panacea and route to inner peace. He shares:

> And you will be drawn in, if you are drawn in, not by desire for gain or
> ease, but simply because at that moment, when the cup was so near your
> lips, you cannot bear to be thrust back again into the cold outer world.

Being in the in-group can be seductive, but ultimately, does it limit our opportunities for growth and development? The implication is that it is easy for people to be drawn into behaving badly and small acts of compromise can lead to an irrevocable position where values are compromised. In research I undertook in 2015 for a postgraduate diploma. I looked at individual motivation in system leadership in the UK Health Service. It was a complex piece of work, my first real experience of thematic analysis, but the summary can be simply condensed to the fact toxic systems create an environment where good people do bad things.

So, what does all this mean when we relate it to race and difference? Racism is real and it does harm. In some cases, racism is explicit and obvious, a possible reaction to the scarcity mindset and the social construct of Other as a risk to one's way of life. Sometimes it is much more beneath the surface.

Most people, however, would not like to think of themselves as racist. At a societal level, we pretend it doesn't exist. It causes discomfort. Most people would rather we didn't talk about it and, all too often, individuals are encouraged to stay quiet; not make a fuss; not be over-sensitive. In my work, I have come across scores of people who were made to feel it was their problem. One community worker, having been called a "Paki" while providing care was upset when she returned to her office. She was told by her manager it was going to happen and maybe she needed to go on a resilience course, the implication being she needed to learn to cope with it. The woman in question was then further insulted by the manager making an inaccurate generalisation about Muslim women. This had a significantly negative impact on the individual, but the manager I am sure felt she did nothing wrong. Her version of empathy was not what was needed in that moment.

Where people from majority groups are sensitive to the issues, sadly all too often they are prevented from being true allies by fear, largely the fear of saying or doing the wrong thing. On a programme I designed called "Conversations Across Difference", the feeling described by the largest number of the majority group is fear: fear of getting it wrong or saying the wrong thing and of the risks this might bring. And so, collectively, in society, we stay silent.

Our natural inclination to Other does lead us, all too often, into thoughtlessly making remarks or behaving in a way which causes hurt and harm. For those on the receiving end, this can lead to a weathering or often imperceptible erosion of self, caused by what are known as "micro-aggressions". Hopper (2019) defines micro-aggressions as "a subtle behaviour – verbal or non-verbal, conscious or unconscious – directed at a member of a marginalized group that has a derogatory, harmful effect". The important thing here is it is about effect or impact. Insult may not have been intended but the negative impact is experienced and undeniably real. The effect of micro-aggressions is cumulative and so often a negative reaction is viewed as an over-reaction, adding fuel to the constructed narrative that it is people of colour who are the problem. Hopper specifically mentions the invalidation of micro-aggressions and the fact this leads to a tendency for people to be seen as over-sensitive. In my work on inclusion, one of my favourite resources to share with participants is a video which likens micro-aggressions to mosquito bites. One is tiresome, dozens have a substantial and debilitating impact. Examples of micro-aggressions are questions about where you are really from, comments about how well you speak English and generalisations based on race. Another example I often hear in my work is confusing you with someone else in an organisation or workplace with a similar ethnic identity. No, we really don't all look the same!

The impact of Othering can escalate into global level conflict. One example is the increasing polarisation of Muslim vs anti Muslim communities. Obaidi, Thomsen and Bergh (2018) explored the concept of "meta- cultural threat". This is a community view that the opposing paradigm poses a substantial threat to their culture and way of life. They describe how this threat elicits a stress response and a subsequent lowering of the threshold to resort to violence on both sides. We see this playing out in many nation states, with both sides attributing blanket negative characteristics to the Other. Ironically in this case, the researchers conclude: "Those who perceive Muslim or Western culture as an inferior, incompatible cultural threat, and endorse violence against it, may have much in common (in terms of psychological processes) with the extremists they hate on the other side."

We see this too in the Russian and Chinese versus the West polarisation and hostility, and in the tragic escalation between Israel and Palestine. Each side is convinced they are right and their version of the truth should prevail. The ultimate expression of Othering is genocide, still unbearably common in many parts of the world.

Global Movement of People

Anthropologists who have studied the evolution of human behaviour in Palaeolithic people talk of the importance of groups as we moved from hunter gatherers who had little control over the environment to settlers who formed communities and learned to grow crops and keep livestock.

As society evolved rapidly, it appears we quickly arrived at an optimal size for groups, where there were enough people to allow division of labour within the new tribes or communities. We are, by nature, social animals, and we release feel good hormones such as serotonin and oxytocin when we sense we belong. This is a direct result of the evolutionary advantage offered by being part of a small, tight-knit community.

There also emerged a complex interaction where neighbouring tribes or communities were seen as a potential threat or as a source of cooperation. Human communities 12,000 years ago in terms of social psychology were arguably not that different to us now. Our social conditioning, which leads us to view other groups as a threat or as a source of resources to be appropriated, was, and remains, well embedded in our social structures.

Indeed, it is this very ideology that led to colonialism and its consequences. Mehta (2019) coined the powerful phrase "we are here because you were there", spelling out the inevitable link between immigration from former colonies and the imperialistic past of Western nations. Some would argue they were a civilising influence, but whether we want to call it imperialism or colonialism, the reality is it was largely about power and money, and it resulted in sizeable seizure of resources. Mehta reminds us that 40 per cent of world borders were created by two countries: Britain and France, in many cases arbitrarily, placing tribes and communities with long standing feuds and conflicts into the same country. This is a major contributory factor to political destabilisation and violence to this day, particularly in the African subcontinent. He is pragmatic in his hope which is for this history to be acknowledged, stating: "I am not calling for open borders. I am calling for open hearts." He gives heartbreaking examples in his book *This Land Is Our Land*, including the border between the US and Mexico as an example of where people came to hold the hands of their separated relatives, the slightest touch offering some solace in a tragic divide.

He also talks of the rushed partition at the end of British rule in India, the outcome of which was directly attributable to the British military and political strategy of divide and rule. By pitting the largely nationalist Hindus and the Muslims against each other for decades, they prolonged their grip on power, and created the conditions where Muslims did not trust they would be safe in a Hindu-ruled state. This led to the calls for independent Muslim states, now Pakistan and Bangladesh.

The impact of the partition of India, Pakistan and Bangladesh was huge, with an estimated one million killed and fifteen million displaced. The scale is inconceivable. My own realisation of the pain of partition came when I watched Deepa Mehta's 1998 film *Earth*. The dramatisation of friends turned against each other by the irresistible force of violence which swept India in 1947 is a very visceral way to understand the scale of the inhumanity, unleashed by lines on a map which were drawn in a five-week period by the British elite.

Mass migration is one of the most significant issues of our time, fuelled by fear and misinformation. We see many people driven to concern and led to believe a protection of borders is the most significant issue of our time. This is arguably cynically fuelled by right-wing media and politicians for whom it is convenient, ignoring the fact that Western states have in the past had very little regard for the borders of other nations. We have short memories and so we fail to make connections to our past, allowing political expedience to be gained by dehumanising people and making Others the problem. A deflection technique perhaps to justify a chronic lack of investment in our core societal infrastructure of health services, transport, housing and education.

In my work with refugee women for a major international charity, I didn't find people who were taking advantage and who were taking a disproportionate level of resources. They were waiting over two years for asylum decisions, leaving them and their families in limbo. Yes, they had access to housing and some healthcare, but they were being asked to live on a weekly budget which most UK-born citizens would regard as a pittance.

In the most extreme case, the dignified woman in front of me, attempting to put her life back together, had fled the country having witnessed her husband killed with a machete in front of her for having different political views to those in power. When I hear some members of the general public interviewed about the 2023 migrant situation saying they should come with papers, it fills me with sadness and quiet rage. Would you stop to find your passport in that situation? Did the Afghan staff who worked alongside the British have time to go back and get their passports when the Taliban brutally and swiftly took the country in 2021? Of course not. In June 2023, I saw a female squadron leader interviewed, for a television documentary *Evacuation*, about the deep trauma of being involved in the airport evacuation in August 2021. Women pleaded with her to take their children. Who could forget the images of people desperate not to be left to their fate, hanging on to the outside of the last UK military plane out of Kabul, falling to their deaths. This is the reality of the situation people in many nations find themselves in. And yet the narrative is all too often about economic migrants, criminal gangs and too many resources taken up by them, the "Other".

Imbalance of Power

As the very term Othering came out of an examination of post-colonialism, it is not surprising that the concept has found itself popping up regularly in discourse on racism. It can be argued that racism is enacted through a combination of prejudice and power, generally reinforcing institutional power, however, this seems to me to have been misdirected in an unhelpful way. It leads to the assertion that people of colour cannot be racist.

If that is where the current epistemological thinking on what racism is gets us to, controversial I know, but I would suggest it needs updating. Of course, I do not deny the particular and systemic legacy of slavery and colonialism, but it feels we now need to be more nuanced in how we consider prejudice and the use of power over, particularly at a macro geo-political level. The elite of middle eastern countries such as Saudi Arabia, Qatar and the UAE have brown skin but have societal and positional power which they use intentionally to hold onto that power, often by Othering those it does not see as full citizens. In my coaching, I worked with a young doctor seeking work in the UK. He was born in Saudi Arabia to a Saudi woman and Yemeni father. On his identify card, under occupation, it says "son of Saudi", even though he was a qualified doctor. His whole identity referenced by his relationship to a person considered of true Saudi blood left him feeling what he characterised as homeless and stateless. I didn't ask him the question directly, but I suspect he felt Othered.

It feels like we need to reframe our language to conceptualise the marginalisation in a different way, and be more nuanced in our judgements. I love Jenny Garrett's (2023) description of black, brown, Asian and mixed heritage individuals as the "global majority". We are not under-represented. We form the majority of world citizens and, while I do not believe GDP as a measure of success is sustainable, if you look at real rates of growth in the last few years, India and parts of Africa and South America tend to be growing much faster than more established economies. Might this start to achieve a shifting of the tectonic plates?

The world in the mid-2020s is turning to the political right and this is evident in the actions and words of a number of leaders. They have emboldened those who peddle hate by legitimising the dehumanisation and disempowerment of Others. They legitimise the explicit language of hate, and certainly in the US, have shifted the dial on the perceived significance of true democracy. They play on fear in a very intentional way in order to promulgate their world view, because of course, in their view, they are right.

Thomas-Olalde and Velho (2011) state: "the 'Others' are constructed through certain practices of knowledge production which legitimise domination". Their view is there is little awareness rather:

> in most cases, these acts of Othering are not perceived as acts of injustice, discrimination or violence, but as unquestioned normality, as natural realities which are legitimately voiced, cast into legislation or turned into actions. We do not generally know the "Other". It is not even about liking or disliking. We generalise in order to reduce our anxiety about social upheaval and to hold onto our perceived power.

And what then of gender? Riyal (2019) in her critique of "Post-Colonialism and Feminism" recrafts colonialism with the following assertion:

> a small but important group of critics has emerged and have attempted to reinterpret colonial encounters or conflicts between colonizers and colonized persons as a struggle between two opposing and intertwined forms of male centrism. In this kind of struggle, women in the colonial master country and women in the colonized country became the victims and symbolic intermediaries of the struggle between the opposing men, and also the objects they used together.

While in the past, this may have been a plausible critique, this suggests a passivity which feels less relevant in current times. It does, however, reinforce the idea that much conflict and inequity in the world is directly related to the male ego.

In my work in leadership, I often refer to the work of Caroline Perez (2019) in her wonderfully powerful book *Invisible Women*. In this book, she outlines with countless examples the inextricable truth that the world is designed by men for men. My personal favourite, which I often use as an example in my work on women's leadership, is about a municipality in Sweden called Karlskoga. Here they discovered that the Snow Clearing Committee, which was made up entirely of working-age men, would prioritise those roads which would have the snow cleared every winter. They chose the main arterial roads, because the men, largely, drove out of the town to work. The roads where women walked their children to school, however, were not cleared. When they investigated they found a high number of accidents amongst pedestrians and cyclists. The men on the Committee did not deliberately set out to disadvantage the women and those using public transport. They simply didn't think about them.

In offering this, I do not mean to Other men or to diminish their contribution to shifting the human paradigm. I merely suggest that, in the same way as we cannot deny the structural inequity caused by race, we also cannot deny the inequity inbuilt into most societies created by male power.

When it comes to Othering, it could be argued that women of colour face a "double whammy". This is expressed in inter-connected stories in Evaristo's 2019 book *Girl, Woman, Other*. She shares the subtle, or not so subtle, ways in which black women must fight to achieve their hopes and dreams. She creates flawed, but strong, characters who draw us into their lived experiences. The final words of her book are: "we should celebrate that many more women are reconfiguring feminism and that grassroots activism is spreading like wildfire and millions of women are waking up to the possibility of taking ownership of our world as fully-entitled human beings". What a powerful and hope generating statement!

When we think about power, over the last century, the rights of children have changed significantly for the better. In the northern hemisphere, it is no longer acceptable to send 12-year-old children to work. Despite assertions of checks and balances, all too often, however, we hear it is still happening in other countries in order to make big global corporations richer. In our desire for cheap goods, clothes and electronic items, we collectively choose not to think about how they are produced.

Where the opportunity for children to be children is undoubtedly improved, again there is an inequality in this. In their seminal work on the adultification of black children, Epstein, Blake, and Gonzzlez (2017) demonstrated that if you are black and a child, there is a distorted perception. In their survey looking at perceptions of white and black girls aged 5–14, they found the following perceptions in a range of interviewees including teachers and police officers:

Black girls need less nurturing
Black girls need less protection
Black girls need less support
Black girls need less comfort
Black girls are more independent
Black girls know more about adult topics
Black girls know more about sex

It is not hard to see that this can have far-reaching and harmful effects on black women. This is particularly significant as the views in this research are held by people who are a fundamental part of the state system and who have "power over" or institutional power over groups or communities. The case of Child Q, who was taken out of an exam in the UK in 2020 and strip-searched while she was on her period, with no appropriate adult, should shock us all. I struggle to comprehend how we as a society have come to think it is acceptable for police to behave in that way.

This is not going to be solved overnight, but again, the more we are aware of the assumptions we make, the more we can actively challenge them, both in unconscious conclusions we come to and in challenging systemic issues. Early in 2023, I was coaching a black school nurse in inner city London who described being exhausted by constantly having to argue against the criminalisation of young black children in case conferences. Her absolute fear was that, if she wasn't there, a child's life chances could be irrevocably damaged. Quite a burden for one individual to carry. She worked very long hours, filling in for vacant staff positions to ensure there was a school nurse presence as often as possible. Not surprising then that she had significant periods of sick leave.

The Scarcity Mindset

Kashtan (2014) highlights that humanity has limited its thinking of how we organise society to largely two views: Communism and neo-liberalism form the polarities of how most nation states choose to be. In so-called democratic society, we have elevated the role of money to king and kingmaker. From when our children can first walk and perceive, they are bombarded with advertising aimed at one thing: encouraging them to consume.

The irony is all this consumerism is not having a positive impact. Schwartz (2004) argues in his aptly named book *The Paradox of Choice* that at one level the concept of choice is deeply attractive as it promotes our sense of autonomy. He also concludes, however, "there comes a point at which opportunities become so numerous that we feel overwhelmed. Instead of feeling in control, we feel unable to cope". The world we have created, which incidentally is destroying the planet, where so much focus is on acquiring material goods, is not making us happy. It is making us feel anxious and is reducing our sense of control.

We are led to believe that if we just have a bigger house or a car with a certain badge, we will somehow be happy and fulfilled. The big business that fuels this desire needs us to keep consuming and so we are sold the fallacy that we can never have enough. This, in turn, promulgates "the scarcity mindset", encouraging us not only to keep spending, but to build real and metaphorical walls.

This is relevant to the inclusion agenda in that we are encouraged to believe there is only one pie and if we give up a slice of pie there is less for us. This plays out in the narrative about migrants. They are taking our jobs and benefits, or they are overwhelming our NHS are common themes in national newspapers and they permeate society, our schools and workplaces. We cannot afford to house them in hotels, so we have to put them on soulless barges, designed for only short-term use. I can only imagine how traumatic it must be for someone who has had a life-threatening journey across the channel to then be escorted back onto the undulating, unpredictable ocean.

A notable observation is the fact many right-of-centre business people and politicians in the UK in 2023 are from South Asian backgrounds. Never before have we had a more ethnically diverse and divisive Cabinet. In some ways, it seems ironic that the offspring of immigrants can take such an anti-immigrant stand, but could it be they are in "the scarcity mindset"? They have been successful and reaped the financial rewards and status. Now, however, they appear to be pulling up the ladder for others, not only colluding, but pushing the boundaries of the narrative that somehow "they" are the problem to ever more extreme language and action. In autumn 2023, the then UK Home Secretary, a woman of South Asian origin, talked of the opposition's plans making Britain a "dumping ground", for millions of immigrants. She also talked of flights taking immigrants to Rwanda as her "dream" and "obsession". This was further stoked by a narrative at the Conservative Party Conference, in the same period, of communities living in parallel in some parts of the UK, the Others, not integrating. This was presented as a problem which was a risk to the very fabric of society. Who, I wonder, are the "in-group" they think they are appealing to?

If we could shift our thinking to "the abundance mindset", genuinely believing there is enough for everybody, how different would our approach be? This is not an idealistic, unrealistic proposition. We have blinkered ourselves into believing that neo-liberalism and communism at the two polarities are the only way to organise society. This is simply not true, and the rise in degrowth economic thinking is unsurprisingly resisted by the status quo but gaining in momentum. The World Economic Forum in June 2022 defined degrowth in the following way:

> Degrowth broadly means shrinking rather than growing economies, so we use less of the world's energy and resources and put wellbeing ahead of profit.
>
> (Masterson, 2022)

They offer practical ways that we can do this without reverting to living in caves. I myself, having moved to a rural setting, find myself swapping goods much more with neighbours, without financial transactions. This feels surprisingly liberating. Twist (2003), in her powerful book *The Soul of Money*, reminds us: "Money is an invention, a distinctly human invention. It is a fabrication of our genius." She goes on to eloquently describe her insights gleaned from 40 years of international fundraising. She introduces us to the concept of "sufficiency", a place where we know we have enough and we make intentional choices based on a different definition of value. Again we come back to the fact an abundance mindset, rather than a scarcity mindset, is possible, sustainable and ultimately allows us to lead happier lives. There is a real choice, a choice which arguably could overcome what Schwartz (2004) calls the "tyranny" of choice.

Of course, the very concept of degrowth economics fundamentally challenges traditional power. It is, therefore, a choice which is ridiculed by those who are focussed on maintaining the status quo at any cost. A very deliberate campaign of attack has been mobilised. We only have to look at the vitriol aimed at Greta Thunberg after her speeches to the UN Climate Summit in 2019. Presidents, politicians and media personalities came out to mock a 16-year-old girl. The feedback included nasty comments about her appearance as well as her views; a suggestion she should be worrying more about her make up than the future of the planet.

The 2021 film *Don't Look Up*, written by Adam McKay, is a masterful piece of satire I would recommend to anyone. This film parodies the response of politicians and global business to the threat of a comet strike on earth, a veiled parallel with the broader biodiversity crisis. Sadly, the film does not end well. Hopefully, the reality can be more positive in terms of the choices we now make.

Hickel et al. (2022) discuss the need for us to find a degrowth paradigm, as the current model of constant growth becomes less achievable in our unstable times. They identify five steps or strategies we need to adopt globally to rebalance and accelerate our progress in decarbonisation, while maintaining justice and wellbeing. They are:

■ **Reduce less-necessary production** – scaling down production and demand for mass produced meat and dairy, fast fashion, cars etc.

- ■ **Improve public services** – they argue good, publicly funded services can produce good outcomes for reasonable cost.
- ■ **Introduce a green jobs guarantee** – this involves initiatives to encourage
  people to train in ecologically advanced technology and to transition from
  polluting industries.
- ■ **Reduce working time** – this has been trialled in some Scandinavian countries.
  It is shown to reduce carbon emissions and free up time for socially focussed
  activities.
- ■ **Ensure sustainable development** – this it is argued required some international debt to be written off, but a focus on supporting industry which con-
  tributes to social value is required.

If the political will is there, many of these proposed solutions are doable. Understand-
ably, politicians are nervous of taking an approach of degrowth or sustainable growth,
which goes so against the grain of what they have been taught are absolute economic
truths. Their focus is likely to be on getting elected or indeed re-elected. The more
communities coalesce and send clear messages, the greater the chances of a shift.

The Ancient Amygdala

There is a deep interrelationship between our social and biological evolution, which,
in recent years, we are only just beginning to understand due to advances in neuroscience. Arguably, our brains have not caught up in evolutionary terms with our
huge technical and social advances and the way we now live. The amygdala is a structure in the anterior lobe of our brains, and it is important because researchers have
found it is the single most important part of our brain in the consideration of how
we process race. It forms one of the most ancient parts of our brain in evolutionary
terms and is known to be involved in our subconscious responses. The amygdala is
particularly associated with the processing of negative stimuli. Kubota, Banaji and
Phelps (2012) used MRI scanning to investigate the role of the amygdala and other
parts of the cortex by correlating reactions to black and white faces with results on
the Implicit Association Test and blink tests. They found that for those the participants perceived as "Other", the amygdala responds in an automatic way, all too
often with fear and distrust, releasing cortisol, a stress hormone. Interestingly, they
also found an internal battle and regulation process going on in our brains where
other brain structures, mainly the anterior cingulate cortex, question implicit conclusions on race. Our thinking or conscious brain is trying to counter our automatic
assumptions.

In addition, they cited evidence from Stanley et al. (2011) which demonstrated
race preference is linked to trust. White players who showed white preference in an
economic game would choose to invest more with white economic partners than
black partners, despite actual qualifications or competence. The researchers refer to

this as a form of neuroeconomics and argue quantification of the impact may help increase our understanding of how the wiring of our brain affects our social decisions. The consequences of this observed effect in terms of our day-to-day life could be significant, with the probability that individuals frequently make unconscious choices which reinforce social inequity. The search for greater understanding on this topic intuitively feels important.

Hughes et al. (2019) also provided MRI-based evidence of the fact that, as our sensory perception develops very early in life, we develop neural networks that distinguish in-group features more than out-group features. So, the fact individuals from other races become grouped as "they" really is hard-wired into our brains very early on in life. Children by the age of one show preferences for people who are the same colour as those they interact with most.

For me, this reinforces the idea that the solution to societal division based on cultural difference is to bring our views about race from the inaccessible unconscious to the conscious mind. We need to invest time and energy in thinking and talking about racial injustice, not from a place of fear, but from curiosity, compassion and positive intent. We also need to practice internal questioning, noticing and reflecting on the potentially erroneous assumptions our mind creates as a default. When it comes to making assumptions, we all do it; this is not a black or white issue, it is a fundamental human issue.

Fitting In

In my work with people from under-represented groups, the need to "fit in" is often cited. This is linked to a relatively low sense of belonging in an organisation or setting. Not feeling able to bring one's true self to social and workplace interactions results in a reduced sense of wellbeing and engagement.

The concept of "code switching" has its origins in the study of language, but more recently has been applied to the exploration of multiple and complex racial identities. McCluney et al. (2019) characterise code switching as a phenomenon that "involves adjusting one's style of speech, appearance, behaviour, and expression in ways that will optimize the comfort of others in exchange for fair treatment, quality service, and employment opportunities". Molinsky (2007) discusses the psychological challenges of "cross cultural code switching", stressing the emotional labour of adapting to fit with dominant cultural norms. It requires constant scanning, vigilance and adaptation. It also, by its very nature, puts the comfort of others before ourselves.

This is not just behavioural, but can be about physical appearance too. In 2020, the YMCA in their report "Young and Black" found that 49% of black school children felt they needed to change their hair to be more acceptable. They reported that they were told by teachers their natural afro hair was "untidy" or "needed brushing".

This links to the important concept of psychological safety, as belonging and psychological safety are inextricably linked. Edmondson (2018) defines it as a situation where individuals can "speak up with ideas, questions, concerns, or mistakes without fear of being punished, humiliated, or rejected by others". If you do not feel you can be your authentic self in the workplace, you are highly unlikely to feel the level of psychological safety to allow you to fully contribute. If you have grown up feeling different and adopted an unconscious strategy of being as small as you possibly can be, achieving psychological safety in a work setting feels like a harder mountain to climb.

This, combined with the effort of code switching or masking one's identity, may explain why despite many positive action initiatives, the majority of organisations have failed to hit diversity targets.

I was fortunate to meet Amy Edmondson in 2023 and spoke to her about this issue. Her response was that, like in so many areas, when considering racial inequity, the solution was to make it "discussable".

In our volatile, ever-changing world, one could counter-argue the ability to fluidly shift our identities and language is a positive. In some respects, we all adapt and behave differently in different situations. The difference, if you are "different", is, it is not a choice, rather a survival strategy.

Being Nice Is Not Enough

We are naturally conflict avoidant and this is deeply rooted, both in evolutionary terms, and in our individual psyche. In prehistoric times, conflict came with the risk of expulsion from the tribe, which would lead to almost inevitable death. Our experiences of witnessing conflict in the home, in schools and in the workplace can also lead us to conflict avoidance. I am sure we can all think of situations, however, where not having a conversation which is necessary leads to escalation. This is often the case for people in the workplace around the issue of race.

In the programmes I facilitate around inclusion, a common starting point for participants is fear of having the conversation, in particular fear of saying the wrong thing. Almost all of these people are good or kind people. Levy (2023) reflects on this in the space of inclusion. She argues the conflict avoidance related to niceness is hindering progress and creating a false sense of progress. She asserts: "You can be a nice person, and at the very same time, totally ignorant of the needs of others. These honourable traits may harm as much as they help." We need to learn how to use productive conflict to good effect to move us forward. Niceness, while well intentioned, is actually, in my view, helping to maintain the status quo.

Ryde (2019) acknowledges the fact that she has a position from which she views the subject. She shares: "I can never really and thoroughly experience the world from an other-than-white perspective." She also concludes the answer is deep self-awareness and a key requirement is the need to: "admit our culpability more honestly". I have seen this in action in the white response to content sharing the systemic history of racism. Hurt, shame and discomfort may be a necessary pre-cursor to active allyship, and reactions I feel comfortable holding a container for. That is different, however, to blame and I, personally, feel the focus needs to be on individual and institutional actions, as opposed to whiteness being seen as intrinsically tied to "racist". Any work that starts with the intention of making in power groups feel guilty is not, in my view, going to move us forward.

In one programme cohort I facilitated, the overwhelming learning point was sitting quietly rather than in some way addressing or calling out racist behaviour or words in the workplace was as bad as being racist. This insight was enabled by people of colour sharing how they felt when colleagues sat silent. Deep transformational work in this area is possible if we prioritise it. One participant said: "I know now, if I don't speak, I am part of the problem." A challenge in this type of work, however, is that a lot of responsibility is placed on people of colour in these groups to be courageous and share their truths. Time after time, I have seen individuals take this bold step. I have also seen people, for understandable reasons, avoid it.

I remain struck, however, by the power of real multi-faceted stories. This counters the risk of what Chimamanda Ngozi Adiche in her 2009 Ted Talk cites as "The Danger of a Single Story". She makes us laugh when she talks of how her American college roommate asked her questions about her music and she presents the fact she read books where people drank tea and ginger beer and played in the snow in a light-hearted way. Born and brought up in Africa, she had never seen snow! Presented with subtlety, this does not take away from the very serious point that when she was growing up, stories which represented her reality were not told or heard in the mainstream. I strongly believe that storytelling is a powerful tool in moving us forward. We need a broader range of stories to create a richer tapestry, so children see themselves reflected in books and other media.

Racial Trauma

There are plenty of people who deny the existence of "racial trauma". How many of us have heard the phrases, "I don't see colour" or "I treat everyone the same" as a response to discussions around inclusion and equity?

Kinouani (2021) states in her book *Living While Black*, in which she explores black mental health: "the core defining feature of racial trauma frameworks is racism and its various manifestations as the cause of psychological distress". There is increasing evidence that trauma can be intergenerational, passed through stories, the impact of behaviour or biologically, through epigenetics. The idea that inequality and racism cause genetic changes, which can have irreversible impact, is both fascinating and frightening.

There is also an undeniable link between micro-aggressions and racial trauma. By denouncing the existence of racial trauma, in-power communities further exacerbate the impact of systemic inequity.

Weathering is real and we know it affects our physical as well as our mental wellbeing. We also know that there are significant inequalities in health outcomes, based on a complex mix of biology, social factors and treatment, driven by systemic assumptions and actions. The statistics on black maternal death and compulsory mental health detention for black and Asian men, as examples, are stark and irrefutable. The Race and Health Observatory (2021) collated data on race-based inequality in outcome and experience in the UK. In a 2021 report commissioned from The King's Fund by the Observatory, we discover black women are four times more likely to die in pregnancy or childbirth than white women. The Covid pandemic has shown us that when faced with a global novel virus, people of colour are twice as likely to die. People of South Asian origin have a 40 per cent higher chance of dying of cardio-vascular disease. Black African and black Caribbean men are eight times more likely to be subject to compulsory treatment orders in mental health services. I could offer many more examples. Some of this can be explained by genetics, but a significant element is caused by systemic inequality and racism.

Geronimus et al. (2006) share research which shows that dealing with racism elicits a long stress response in both children and adults and this can lead to inflammation and the increased prevalence of chronic disease. It is linked to the increased production of cortisol. This, in turn, leads to an increase in mortality and a greater percentage of people living with life limiting disability. The burden of racism is literally making us ill.

Kiles et al. (2021) described the consequence of racial trauma following the death of George Floyd in 2020 amongst a group of black pharmacy and medical students in the US as "hyperawareness of surroundings, relationships, and action/ inaction of peers and institutions". They talked of "vicarious trauma, hypervigilance, and fight or flight responses", all causing significant distress and physiological stress. This, inevitably, led to them having to work harder to achieve, again an externally imposed additional burden related to the accident of their birth.

A fact sheet produced by the Association of Behavioural and Cognitive Therapists identifies the following lengthy list of conditions or behaviours linked to racial trauma:

■ depression
■ anxiety
■ headaches
■ upset stomach or gastrointestinal issues
■ humiliation
■ difficulty sleeping
■ nightmares
■ loss of appetite
■ hypervigilance
■ crying spells
■ difficulty concentrating
■ low self-esteem
■ avoidance behaviours.

In my work, I have seen racial trauma play out with individuals who have clearly been harmed by their previous experiences. My personal challenge is that these are some of the hardest people to work with. I feel so much empathy and yet, on occasions, when doing difficult and deep work, have felt the target of their projected pain in ways that have felt extremely uncomfortable and which, in some cases, have been very hurtful.

Menakem (2017) states: "Our very bodies house the unhealed dissonance and trauma of our ancestors." He identifies trauma as not entirely negative, but a protective mechanism, linked to our mechanism to fight, flee or freeze. The frozen state is where we can get stuck in a trauma response. In this space, we cannot think rationally and will often act in ways others might see as irrational. Menakem's book *My Grandmother's Hands* is essentially a book about healing. He identifies that healing is not binary, but we can move in the right direction, through a series of mind and body practices. He identifies the concepts of "clean" and "dirty" pain. Clean pain is associated with stepping into the unknown and a capacity for growth, whereas dirty pain is what he describes as "the pain of avoidance, blame and denial".

Hypervigilance is commonly cited in investigations of racial trauma. The constant scanning for behaviours or situations that take individuals back to difficult experiences is undoubtedly exhausting. It can, also, lead to inaccurate perceptions that any difference in view expressed by others is related to race. This is so complex and emotive and can counter against the ability of people to have the generative conversations that will move things forward.

I feel the anxiety in me rise as I write this. So much of what women of colour express is the negative effect of not being heard and I feel nervous about anything that could be construed as denying their reality. Can we hold the compassion and still hold the view that an individual's constructed reality may be very different from that of others and indeed our own personal perceptions? I am not sure the current models fully support practitioners in trying to do this challenging work. The following comment from Kinouani's 2021 book really resonated for me: "there is a level of communication, which is unseen and unconscious or pre-verbal, that neither black employees, white employers nor structures are adequately equipped for or willing to explore".

I am left curious as to how we can equip ourselves better in this space. Kinouani's work moves us forward, but I am wanting so much more. If I am honest, my experiences in recent years have sometimes led me to want to shy away from this work. I could choose to do work which is so much easier. I am trying to hold myself in the discomfort in order to grow and understand and, hopefully in my own small way, contribute to moving us forward.

Sue et al. (2019) identify a positive response to trauma, discussing the use of "microinterventions", to counter the micro-aggressions. They identify four major strategic goals of microinterventions:

■ make the invisible visible
■ disarm the microaggression
■ educate the perpetrator
■ seek external reinforcement or support

Making the invisible visible is not an easy task in busy organisations, but what needs to follow is an active process, which requires focus, resource and an environment where all are prepared to reflect and learn.

Increasingly, those working in the area of racial justice argue that the work to be done to overcome racial trauma needs to go beyond the cognitive and into the somatic. I am interested in the work of organisations such as Healing Justice, who argue that a somatic or body-focussed approach is required to reconnect to our whole selves. What distinguishes racial trauma from other types of trauma-related disorders is the ongoing and pervasive effect. To overturn the subsequent learned behaviour arguably requires a shift in life practice which many don't have access to, are unaware of or are unwilling to embrace. My hope is we can encourage more individuals to step into this place of healing.

Can Humans Be "We" Not "I"?

Social psychology clearly purports that identity as socially constructed. This is interwoven with our increasing understanding of the biological basis of behaviour at a neural, endocrine or epigenetic level. Our identity is fluid and, perhaps, when we consider recent advances in our awareness of neuroplasticity, more fluid than we may have thought.

Although there is a good theoretical argument that humans developed bias and Othering as a survival technique, we are substantially evolved as a species and cannot use our biological and social wiring as an excuse. Agarwal (2020) states: "discussion of the evolutionary basis of cognitive biases does not give us permission to behave in discriminatory ways". I wholeheartedly agree!

As we reflect on how we might shift society, it feels like a priority is the move from "I" to "we". How likely are we to be able to achieve this aim and to unlearn the conditioning which drives an ego-centric approach?

Sedikides et al. (2013) talked of the identity of self-concept being made up of three connected but unequal dimensions: the individual self, the relational self and the collective self. The individual self is self-explanatory relating to one's individual uniqueness, the relational self relates to dyadic bonds, relationships that matter with individuals who are close and the collective self relates to self in wider society. They argue that the individual self, particularly in situations of threat, takes primacy. It might feel like an uncomfortable truth that when it comes down to it; self is more important than those around us. For those of us who want to believe in society as a force for good and a sense of our collective humanity transcending the needs and wants of individuals, this feels particularly counter to what we want to be true.

Nancy Kline in her work has a more hopeful view of our capacity to transcend our limited thinking and connection. Her ten components of the Thinking Environment often form a plank of my work with groups and I have completed a Foundation Course in the Thinking Environment. In her 2020 book *The Promise That Changes Everything* she speaks of Component Eight: Difference. She suggests our inability to deal with difference with open hearts limits human thinking. She also states: "difference is often so deeply threatening we cannot bear to listen to it. Much less embrace it. We cannot bear to imagine that we might be wrong or they might be right and, heaven forbid, at least as good in every way as we are. Or better."

We go back to the cognitive process of social comparison as a key vehicle by which we build and maintain self-esteem.

The late Judith Glaser, cited in Balbao and Glaser (2018) also had a more positive view, creating the concept of "Conversational Intelligence". They build on her work and identify that the following should be our focus if we are to move to a more positive sense of "we" rather than "I".

7 Dimensions

- Co-Creating: working together to move from I to WE.
- Humanising: trusting, respecting, appreciating, and honouring Others with an openness to have difficult conversations with candor and care.
- Aspiring: expanding dreams and aspirations with Others to be able to achieve greatness.
- Navigating: sharing ideas, information and breaking down silos to collaborate across boundaries.
- Generating: discovering next generation thinking by opening the space for testing, experimenting, challenging the status quo, and asking "what if" questions.
- Expressing: developing the leadership voice in Others, including being able to speak up and push back on authority.
- Synchronising: measuring and celebrating success; focusing on milestones, and ways to capture progress toward achieving shared goals.

This sounds an eminently sensible list, but I am left feeling a big gap on the how. What do we as concerned humans and practitioners need to do to make this happen? What does "humanising" look like in reality?

More specifically related to race, Garrett (2023), in her book, introduces the model ADEPT to help us through a journey. The phases are:

Expanding our **A**wareness of the context
          Deepening our knowledge of lived-experience
    Being an **E**mpathetic changemaker
   Defining our **P**athways to action
    Practising **T**houghtful introspection

Conversational intelligence fundamentally connects to the concept of generative conversations; conversation as a tool to create new knowledge and insight. Osborne and Hinson (2015) describe generative conversations in the following way: "Generative conversations are conversations that generate new value or meaning."

This also links to the concept of sensemaking. The ability to find space to go beyond our normal boundaries and create meaning in new ways feels vital. Ancona (2011) states: "sensemaking calls for courage, because while there is a deep human need to understand and know what is going on in a changing world, illuminating the change is often a lonely and unpopular task".

In our world of increasing eco and social anxiety, where war is now, once again, viewed as normal, there is a natural mechanism which orients us towards paralysis. How do we move from this denial to active processing, connection, sensemaking and taking responsibility? And how then to we move to action?

My belief is that we need to find a way to have generative conversations. Lovely though it may feel to have an echo-chamber of like-minded people to connect to, I am now trying to be more intentional about how I use my time. It will require courage and stepping into discomfort personally, but my commitment is that I will try and have more conversations with people with very different views and try and understand, not judge. Easier said than done, I know.

We need fundamental transformation; we need to find a different way of living to deal with our existential challenges and, all too often across the world, I would suggest the kernels of hope are coming from women.

Joanna Macy and Chris Johnstone are founders of *The Work That Reconnects* (*Coming Back to Life: The Updated Guide to The Work that Reconnects*, 2014). Joanna talks of active hope stating:

> Whatever the limitations of our life, we are still free to choose which version of reality – or story about our world – we value and want to serve.
> We can choose to align with business as usual, the unravelling of living systems, or the creation of a life-sustaining society.

She reminds us that we still have that choice. We have the technology to live very differently, in a way which does not destroy all that keeps us alive on this planet.

If we are collectively able to make the right choices, what might a life-sustaining society mean for inclusivity?

References

ABCT (n.d.) Race Based Traumatic Stress. Race-Based Traumatic Stress | Fact Sheet – ABCT – Association for Behavioral and Cognitive Therapies (Accessed 17 September 2023).

Agarwal, P. (2020) *Unravelling Unconscious Bias*. London: Bloomsbury.

Ancona, D. (2011) Sensemaking: Framing and Acting in the Unknown. In Snook, P., Nohria, N. and Khurana, R. (eds) *The Handbook for Teaching Leadership*. Los Angeles: Sage Publications.

Assche, J. V., Politi, E., Van Dessel, P. and Phalet, K. (2020) To Punish Or to Assist? Divergent Reactions to Ingroup and Outgroup Members Disobeying Social Distancing. *British Journal of Social Psychology*, 59(3): 571–789.

Balboa, N. and Glaser, R. D. (2018) The Neuroscience of Conversations. www.psychologytoday.com/gb/blog/conversational-intelligence/201905/the-neuroscience-of-conversations (Accessed 15 May 2023).

Berger, P. and Luckmann, T. (1966) *The Social Construction of Reality: A Treatise in the Sociology of Knowledge.* New York: Doubleday.

Chimamanda Ngozi Adiche (2009) The Danger of a Single Story. www.youtube.com/watch?v=D9Ihs241zeg (Accessed 15 May 2023).

Don't Look Up (2021) Directed by Adam Kay. Bluegrass Films.

Earth (1998) Directed by Deepa Mehta. Hamilton Mehta Productions.

Edmondson, A. (2018) *The Fearless Organization: Creating Psychological Safety in the Workplace for Learning, Innovation, and Growth.* London: Cornerstone Press.

Epstein, R., Blake, J. J. and Gonzzlez, T. (2017) Girlhood Interrupted: The Erasure of Black Girls' Childhood www.researchgate.net/publication/319562840_Girlhood_Interrupted_The_Erasure_of_Black_Girlss_Childhood (Accessed 4 August 2023).

Evaristo, B. (2019) *Girl, Woman, Other.* New Jersey: John Wiley & Sons.

Garrett, J. (2023) *Equality vs Equity.* Leeds: Emerald Publications.

Geronimus, A. T., Hicken, M., Keene, D. and Bound, J. (2006) "Weathering" and Age Patterns of Allostatic Load Scores Amongst Blacks and Whites in the United States. *American Journal of Public Health*, 96(5): 826–833.

Hickel, J., Kallis, G., Jackson, T., O'Neill, D. W., Schor, J. B., Steinberger, J. K., Victor, P. A. and Urge-Vorsatz, D. (2022) Degrowth Can Work – Here's How Science Can Help. *Nature*, 12 December. www.nature.com/articles/d41586-022-04412-x (Accessed 12 January 2024).

Hopper, E. (2019) What Is a Micro-aggression? Everyday Insults with Harmful Effects. www.thoughtco.com/microaggression-definition-examples-4171853 (Accessed 5 July 2023)

Hughes, B. L. (2019) Neural Adaptation to Faces Reveals Racial Outgroup Homogeneity Effects in Early Perception https://pubmed.ncbi.nlm.nih.gov/31262811/ (Accessed 12 January 2024).

James, M. and Burgos, A. (2022) Race. In Zalta, E. N. (ed.) *The Stanford Encyclopedia of Philosophy.* https://plato.stanford.edu/archives/spr2022/entries/race/ (Accessed 23 June 2023).

Kashtan, M (2014) *Reweaving the Human Fabric: Working Together to Create a Nonviolent Future*, Oakland, CA: Fearless Heart Publication.

Kiles, T. M., Cernasev, A., Tran, B. and Chisholm-Burns, M. (2021) Effects of Racial Trauma on Black Doctor of Pharmacy Students. *Am J Pharm Educ.*, 85(9): 8558. doi: 10.5688/ajpe8558. PMID: 34301549

Kinouani, G. (2021) *Living While Black: The Essential Guide to Overcoming Racial Trauma.* London: Penguin Random House.

Kline, N. (2020) *The Promise That Changes Everything.* London: Penguin Random House.

Kubota, J. T., Banaji, M. R. and Phelps, E. A. (2012) The Neuroscience of Race. *Nature Neuroscience*, 15: 940–948.

Levy, S. (2023) *Mind the Inclusion Gap.* London: Unbound.

Lewis, C. S. (1944) *The Inner Ring: The 1944 Memorial Lecture at King's College.* https://archive.org/details/1944-the-inner-ring/page/4/mode/2up (Accessed 5 July 2023)

Macy, J. and Brown, M. (2014) *Coming Back to Life: The Updated Guide to The Work that Reconnects.* British Columbia: New Society Publishers.

Masterson, V. (2022) Degrowth – What's Behind the Economic Theory and Why Does it Matter Right Now? World Economic Forum. 15 June. www.weforum.org/agenda/2022/06/what-is-degrowth-economics-climate-change/ (Accessed 12 January 2024).

McCluney, C. L., Robotham, K., Lee, S., Smith, R. and Durkee, M. (2019) The Cost of Code Switching. https://hbr.org/2019/11/the-costs-of-codeswitching (Accessed 12 January 2024).

Mehta, S. (2019) *This Land Is Our Land: An Immigrants Manifesto.* London: Penguin Random House.

Menakem, R. (2017) *My Grandmother's Hands.* Las Vegas: Central Recovery Press.

Molinsky, A. (2007) Cross-Cultural Code-Switching: The Psychological Challenges of Adapting Behavior in Foreign Cultural Interactions. *The Academy of Management Review,* 32(2): 622–640.

Onuf, N. J. (1989) *World of Our Making: Rules and rule in Social Theory and International Relations.* Reissued. Abingdon: Routledge.

Obaidi, M., Thomsen, L. and Bergh, R. (2019). "They Think We Are a Threat to Their Culture": Meta-Cultural Threat Fuels Willingness and Endorsement of Extremist Violence against the Cultural Outgroup. *International Journal of Conflict and Violence,* 12, a647.

Osborne, D. and Hinson, J. (2015) Generative Conversations – Results Through Connection and Meaning. https://change-fusion.com/wp-content/uploads/2015/12/GenerativeConversations.pdf (Accessed 20 May 2023).

Palmer, A. (2017) *Seven Surrenders: Terra Ignota,* Book 2. Chicago: Tom Doherty Associates.

Perez, C. C. (2019) *Invisible Women: Exposing Data Bias in a World Designed for Men.* London: Vintage.

Powell, W. (2018) Object to Subject: Three Scholars on Race, Othering and Bearing Witness. Ed Andrew Grant Thomas. www.otheringandbelonging.org/object-subject-three-scholars-race-othering-bearing-witness/ (Accessed 23 June 2023).

Riyal, A. L. M. (2019) Post Colonialism and Feminism. *Asian Social Science,* 15(11): 83.

Ryde, J. (2019) *White Privilege: Unmasked.* London: Jessica Kingsley Publishers.

Schwartz, B. (2004) *The Paradox of Choice: Why More is Less.* New York: Harper Collins.

Sedikides, C. Gaertner, L., Luke, A. L., O'Mara, E. M. and Gebauer, J. E. (2013) A Three-Tier Hierarchy of Self-Potency: Individual Self, Relational Self, Collective Self. *Advances in Experimental Social Psychology,* 48: 235–295.

Stanley, D. A., Sokol-Hessner, P., Fareri, D. S., Perino, M. T., Delgado, M. R., Banji, M. R. and Phelps, E. A. (2011) cited in Kubota, J. T., Banaji, M. R. and Phelps, E. A. (2012). The Neuroscience of Race. *Nature Neuroscience,* 15: 940–948.

Sue, D. W., Alsaidi, S., Awad, M. N., Glaeser, E., Calle, C. Z. Mendez, N. (2019). Disarming Racial Microaggressions: Microintervention Strategies for Targets, White Allies, and Bystanders. *American Psychologist,* 74(1): 128–142. https://doi.org/10.1037/amp0000296

Tajfel, H., Turner, J. C., Austin, W. G. and Worchel, S. (1979) An Integrative Theory of Intergroup Conflict. In *Organizational Identity: A Reader.* Oxford: Oxford University Press, 56–65.

The Race and Health Observatory (2021) Ethnic Health Inequalities and the NHS. www.nhsrho.org/wp-content/uploads/2023/05/Ethnic-Health-Inequalities-Kings-Fund-Report.pdf (Accessed 15 May 2023)

The Sound of Music (1965) Directed by Robert Wise. 20th Century Studios.

Thomas-Olalde, O. and Velho, A. (2011) Othering and its Effects: Exploring the Concepts. www.academia.edu/42889355/Othering_and_its_effects_exploring_the_concept (Accessed 12 July 2023).

Twist, L. (2003) *The Soul of Money.* New York: Norton & Co.

Weick, K. (1995) *Sensemaking in Organisations.* University of Michigan: Sage Publications.

YMCA (2020) Young and Black. www.ymca.org.uk/wp-content/uploads/2020/10/ymca-young-and-black.pdf (Accessed 15 September 2023).

2

Experience of Being "Other"

A Prelude

In the words of Desmond Tutu: "Exclusion is never the way forward on our shared paths to freedom and justice." I also strongly believe in the concept of taking agency and the words of the great Maya Angelou resonate here with her stating: "You may not control all the events that happen to you, but you can decide not to be reduced by them."

One of the minor frustrations in my life is the fact I often fail identity checks. I cannot renew my driving license online. That is not because I have suspicious activity in my past. (I am not sure being in Youth CND – for those too young to remember, the youth division of the Campaign for Nuclear Disarmament – will be forever held against me.) It is because I find myself with different names on different key documents, such as my passport and driving license. This even became an issue at my daughter's wedding, when the registrar called me in to check names on my birth certificate and passport, which were different. The wedding actually started a few minutes late.

This is as a direct result of something that happened to me over 50 years ago. My birth name was Priti, but at the age of three when I went to a nursery school in my birthplace, Lancaster, the teacher asked my mum if they could call me Rita. I will never know her motivation for this. It may have been with positive intent to stop me being teased. Those were the days before we had a Home Secretary in the UK bear that name in 2019. I can only imagine how it made my parents feel. They had carefully chosen a name for me, and, together with so much of their identity, that too was taken away from them. Priti is thought in Sanskrit to mean joy, grace or favour. I am sure there were many subsequent times where my parents found it hard

DOI: 10.4324/9781003390602-3

to think of me as a gift, particularly in my teenage years, but that was the sentiment they clearly had at my birth.

In many cultures, names carry great significance and meaning, and the giving of a name holds symbolic importance in most societies, often being marked by ritual and family or religious events.

Like many of their peers arriving in England in the '60s and '70s, my parents, however, also adopted "English" names. Born as Praful and Shakuntala, they were also Peter and Sheila.

The idea that something as fundamental as a name can be taken away from human beings is not new, and the act of renaming is an ancient act of the exercise of power. I am very hopeful that what happened to me would not now happen 50 years later, but I suspect subtle acts still pervade. Certainly, our experience of modern life in the northern hemisphere is names of south east Asian or African origin are still often shortened or anglicised. I have learnt names are important, and I always make a point of asking the question if there is a shred of doubt on how to address some-one. My menopausal brain doesn't always remember, so sometimes, sadly, I have to ask more than once. But I ask.

In my study of the experience of being "Other", I had the privilege of interview-ing a number of women of colour, from different backgrounds, including mixed race or dual heritage. There were eight women in total, connected by invisible threads, but all wonderfully unique. For the purposes of anonymity, I have changed their names.

Table 2.1 gives a summary of the study participants, the eight fabulous women who shared a part of their life stories to support me in bringing this book to life. I must admit to some discomfort in putting them in boxes, but this is done with the intent that it makes it easier to understand the context when you come to their stories.

An early realisation struck me as I immersed myself in the data, something that appears obvious, but was somehow startling. The women were all completely differ-ent and unique individuals, with a reality constructed from their life experiences.

Table 2.1 Study Participants

Name	Ethnic Description	Work background
Miki	Anglo-Japanese	Law, facilitation, international development
Suki	South Asian of Indian origin	Local government
Kirsten	Anglo-Caribbean	Professional services
Sadia	Indo-Mauritian	Local government
Nilima	South Asian of Indian origin.	Charity sector
Virginia	Anglo-Caribbean, parents both mixed race	Psychology/ Global HR
Lorella	Afro-Caribbean	Healthcare
Talia	Pakistani/ European	Acting/ leadership development

Had I too, despite the obvious differences in the individuals I spoke with, been drawn into homogenising them? A sober reminder to myself to consider them as distinct individuals and to only generalise from their experiences where the data led me to emergent themes.

From a thematic analysis of their words and their individual stories using a qualitative methodology known as Interpretative Phenomenological Analysis (IPA), I was able to identify themes. This is a method which specifically focusses on sensemaking and on how individuals understand and interpret life events. It felt an appropriate method for what is essentially a narrative rather than a quantitative approach to this exploration. I considered options for how I share the depth of their input to this endeavour. I have chosen to interweave their words in the text to illustrate the themes identified.

Awareness of Difference

For the individuals I spoke to, the age at which they had an awareness that they were different varied. It was very much dependent on whether they formed part of the majority or minority community in which they spent their early years.

For all, there was a sense of being different, which was further processed with hindsight. Sadia stated: "It's only in the latter years, when I looked at culture and felt like when you really dissect it, there was more to growing up than I saw at the time." Talia also shared a similar sense of lack of recognition of difference. Her words were: "As a child growing up in the '70s, you didn't challenge your thoughts or have any kind of thought processes around what was going on in your life ... so for our traditional Sunday lunch we would go and eat curry. It was normal." Sadia described growing up in a suburb of London, stating: "When I got to school there were other Asians in the year, but they weren't necessarily in my group of friends. And so, I actually felt very 'Other' for most of my childhood."

Lorella reflects: "I would have liked more opportunities to talk to my mum, who didn't really want to talk about race or racism; she felt you are British and that you should fit in. She did us a disservice in that respect." "Fitting in" is a common priority and links to concepts of code switching, previously discussed.

Anyone who can remember puberty and the early teenage years will recall how excruciating the process of development into adult is, as a complex interaction of endocrine, that is, biological and social changes, occur in our bodies. We begin to pull away from our parents and form the ability to hypothesise and test our views on life. As we do this, the concept of self as different is likely to be exacerbated.

Phinney (1993) presents a three-stage model of identification of ethnicity in young people.

Stage 1 Unexamined Ethnic Identity
Stage 2 Ethnic Identity Search
Stage 3 Ethnic Identity Achievement

These are not necessarily developmental in a linear way, but she identifies Stage 1, "Unexamined Ethnic Identity" as a state where there has been little consideration of ethnic identity. In the case of our interviewees, this would be us identifying with our white counterparts and not actively reflecting on our difference. In exploring stage 2, "Ethnic Identity Search", young people reach a state where the need to understand the role of ethnicity in ego and self-development is heightened and some active reflection has begun. Stage 3, which is not a goal as such, but is associated with better psychological regulation, is "Ethnic Identity Achievement". This occurs when ethnicity is internalised and forms a comfortable part of individual identity. For some, this state is never achieved.

Sometimes the realisation in adulthood is quite stark. Miki, who had a difficult childhood and moved around frequently, was recently sent some photos by a cousin living abroad. Miki is mixed race, English and Japanese, and so her response to the question about identity was different in that she said: "I don't really fit into a category." Her overriding sense from her childhood, other than a focus on survival, was the feeling she did not belong to a community. In terms of hierarchy of need, perhaps for her with a mother prone to violence due to mental illness and hostile wider family, safety was paramount. This arguably made her less cognisant of her difference, while, at the same time, holding an unconscious confusion. She shared: "It's difficult, because it's this thing about being uncertain all the time, knowing that one is different." Her response, when she looked at the photos of her as a child of four of five, which she had never seen before, was: "I'm quite dark and they are all light skinned. And it's really obvious. It is so obvious, but I don't think I was ever aware of it." So, Miki never felt she belonged to a community based on racial differentials and still doesn't. Upon reflection, she stated: "I can see how things were different for me at school or the places I went to, some of the ways I was treated. But, I didn't really put two and two together until later." She does, however, now see advantages to the fact it is hard to categorise her or put her in a box. She shared: "the advantage of not fitting in is it makes me feel more of an individual".

For others, the rich diversity of their background made it hard to establish a clear identity based on ethnicity. Virginia's parents moved to a part of the UK with few black individuals from the West Indies, but they were both actually of mixed heritage, so a simple sense of identity based on historic race and culture was always going to be difficult for her. She identifies as a "second descendant" and still has a close association with the geography and culture in the UK where she was brought up. She describes little awareness of race until, at the age of 13, she went to visit relatives in the USA. She remembers vividly: "they were really very, very aware of race and colour". For her, it took this experience to shift her into the Ethnic Identity Search phase, described earlier in Finney's model. She became curious and read books, stating: "that made me question – what are my thoughts about my identity and race?" This helped her make sense of and accept who she was.

An understandable strategy in their early years may, in contrast, be a more intentional approach to ignoring ethnicity, race and colour. Talia stated: "For the longest time I was in denial about it, because that was easy." She did not look obviously of mixed Pakistani/European descent and therefore, living in a white middle-class area in the South of England, there was a lack of awareness and consciousness. She stated: "There wasn't anybody who looked like me, but I didn't think anything of it." She described a later awareness that she gravitated towards girls who were different at her large secondary school. She bravely acknowledges her shift: "It was much more unconscious rather than conscious, which is why I think it's been a journey for me to discover my identity, because I have been very good at burying it, because virtually no one would pick up on it." Who can blame any individual who has the choice for not taking on the burden of being the "Other"?

For a few of the women I interviewed, they specifically mentioned a sense of what they were being told by friends not necessarily being true, particularly in relation to their family's views. I remember one friend, Linda, who lived on our street, saying her friends weren't allowed in the house. I accepted this, though was very confused when at the age of about eight, I realised her neighbour, a mutual friend, was allowed to enter. I can only conclude with hindsight that her parents did not want an Asian child in their house.

Suki, in contrast, had a different experience as she was brought up in a predominantly South Asian community, resulting in her being part of the majority community where she grew up. She stated: "I think about my culture and upbringing really positively" so, for her, this gave a sense of belonging and pride. She does not have the same experience of knowing she was different from a very early age, around the subject of race, however, for her, the awareness of difference was around gender. After the age of around five, as the only girl with two brothers, her early recognition was that she was treated differently and had less freedoms than her male siblings. Her awareness of racial difference did not come until well into her teens. She describes being in the majority group as a place of some safety, but has only just in the last few years examined her early years with a more critical lens. She described feeling some guilt at this examined past, but did reflect that she had a disproportionate role in caring duties in the family and a sense that she should put other's needs before her own. This may well have affected the pace at which she developed and progressed at work. She said: "There is a lot that has been ingrained into me that I have absorbed as normal behaviour and has impacted how I think and process and how I engage with others." Suki has clearly done a lot of reflecting, but even now as a senior leader in her fifties, she spoke of the effort she has to put in to give herself permission to challenge older men in a work context.

For others, like Nilima, the awakening around difference was more frightening and aggressive. She described being six or seven and riding her bike on the road, when some "skinheads" shouted at her and spat at her. She was so terrified, she hid in a bush and did not come out for quite a long time, as she feared they would come back. There came the painful and unjust realisation: "So I realised I was different then; that they were picking on me for something I had no control over." She described being the only girl of Indian origin at her school and stated: "I knew I was there and different." Like me, she also does describe the majority of children in primary school being nice and playing with her, but an experience like that does become cemented in your psyche. Sadly, this distress was to be exacerbated by further life experiences, which we will explore later. A telling comment was: "It just felt like you were an alien." Interesting that some countries still call immigrants "illegal aliens". Language, as ever, holds power and meaning.

For Kirsten, of dual heritage, having a mother who was white British with a strong connection to her grandparents meant, in her early years, she did not feel a sense of difference. She shared the shock of moving from a village primary school to a larger school in the local town: "That's when I got spat on going to school and called names. My response was indignant." For her, she described these negative experiences as fuelling her resilience and she commented that "strong minded" was often cited on her school reports! She took agency and, as much as she could, avoided people who were negative towards her. She said: "If you are going to treat me like that, then I'm sorry, but I will go somewhere else where they don't." A strong appreciation of injustice and unfairness linked to a strong sense of self-worth appears to have served her well. Even she, however, described the ongoing impact of prejudice on her current thinking: "If I've been in meetings where I am being ignored, that might be for a hundred and one reasons, but you always assume it's for the same reason as to why you might have been Othered somewhere else."

Lorella, of Afro-Caribbean origin, described being brought up in a Midlands village. She was aware of race, but her earlier memory is of an absent father and her mum bringing up her and her two siblings alone. She did, however, share: "We were the only black family in that community. So the only black children in that primary school. I don't think anyone made an issue of it as such, but I definitely knew I was different and did not fit in." Lorella, in some ways, described her response to racism in a similar way to Kirsten. She did not appear to have her confidence obviously knocked by experiences of racism, rather it created a sense of identity based on the outward show of strength. She shared: "I was treated differently and there was a level of micro-aggression. Most people would not come out and say it, but there was one boy who was very physically aggressive. I behaved like I was confident then. I suppose I wasn't really confident, but I had to present as being confident in order to push back." She does describe, however, that she was "quite comfortable not necessarily being part of a group". She clearly developed her own strategies for navigating her way through her secondary school years which involved a combination of distancing and masking.

For me personally, I think I was about six when I was first called a "Paki": at Ryelands Primary School, in Lancaster. My memories are vague, but I remember being confused and scared, but that may be because the culprit was well known for her shin kicking too. I also remember the kindness of my friend Jane during this incident.

This sense of micro-aggressions being countered by support and kindness is a theme that came up in many of the interviews, with one woman reasoning: "just as you get bad people, you get good people". I have a really clear memory from secondary school of a religious education class around race and one girl in the class, called

Sarah, did share her viewpoint that she did not think coloured people should be here and they should go home. This was probably my first experience of a conversation about race being skilfully facilitated. I forget the name of the teacher. Some of my classmates came up to me at break and asked me how I was and how could I speak to Sarah anymore. I remember the discomfort, but I was left even then, at the age of 13 or 14, feeling it was better to discuss and debate it. She held those views and that was not going to change if they were not voiced and gently challenged.

My observation from speaking to the women is there was very little active dialogue about issues of race in the '60s, '70s and '80s. Talia stated: "It wasn't encouraged to have any thought processes about your identity growing up in the seventies." Rather, it was a subject in the shadows.

Many of the women describe growing up, like myself, in areas where there were small minority communities and we composed one of only a handful of black, Asian or other minority girls in our schools. There is a curious dichotomy which emerged from the research in terms of experience of racism and place. The interviewees who grew up in villages shared a more positive experience compared to, say, Nilima, who grew up in a white suburb of a large multi-cultural city. From listening to the women, I feel possibly this may be explained by consideration of who forms the in-group, in that if we take the initial definition by Brons, in the village, due to the small number of individuals, the in-group was the whole village, and there was no need for further differentiation.

In contrast, Sadia described being in an affluent part of London as a very different, expressing that her community was "This progressive, diverse bubble where you just assume everyone is like you and interacting with really diverse people. But actually, that is so far from the truth and it is probably the opposite for the majority of people."

Where there was more of a sense of integration, race was often still below the surface. How many of us have experienced conversations where others are verbally abused only to be told, "But we don't mean you, you are different", or "You are one of us"? The feelings that induces are complex for young minds to process: relief and guilt inter-twined.

Difference wasn't always related to skin shade but can be linked to other cultural differences. Sadia described feeling Othered as she did not go out to pubs and clubs, as she was a practicing Muslim. She reflected on the alienation of Monday mornings when everyone talked about going out at the weekend to bars and clubs and she could not join in the conversations. She had no relevant experience to bring and this accentuated her difference. It sounds like there was little attempt to bring her into the conversation in a more inclusive way, rather a blinkered world view which didn't notice her exclusion.

In some ways, the reflection on identity needs to be an active process. As many of the individuals I interviewed were in roles in coaching, psychology, development or health and social care, they had all done a lot of thinking about their life story and the shift in self-image and self-esteem they achieved by doing the self-work.

For most of us, it remains a work in progress and always will be.

The Notion of Colour-blindness

How many times do we hear the statement "I don't see race or colour", or, when asked the question about which race people identify with, I was met with the answer, "the human race". This is well intentioned and based on an erroneous view that treating everyone in the same way is the key to equality. What this colour-blindness actually does is allow those with power to deny racism exists and not have to get uncomfortable talking about it. People of colour know race is an issue. They deal with it in their daily lives. Williams (2016) explores how this plays out in our interaction with young children. She describes how parents, even when the topic is racial prejudice, avoid mentioning race explicitly when reading with four- or five-year-olds. Children pick up on this and, by the age of ten, this discomfort at talking about race is well ingrained and affects the behaviour of young people. She also offers practical solutions in her paper for addressing the issue: suggesting: "The answer lies in embracing and celebrating our racial differences instead of minimising or even altogether ignoring them."

The women I interviewed in my study were often left with a profound sense of missing something in their childhood. A number of the women describe a process of active reflection and re-examination of their early years, where there is a realisation that their awareness of dynamics and relationships was somehow blinkered.

For many of the women, the fact race was not discussed did not serve them as they grew into adulthood. Talia shared: "I always had a sense of being different in some way, and I have always had a sense of not being good enough, not fitting in." This has taken a lot of work in adulthood to unpick and move beyond. She described when she started work with the United Nations being told she didn't look of a different colour and told she had a choice of how she presented herself. This led her to the stark realisation that her father had no such choice.

A common theme amongst the interviewees was the active processing in later life to understand themselves, commit to action and practice self-compassion.

Williams (2016) argues rather than ignoring race, one solution is to celebrate racial diversity early on. She suggests working with the natural curiosity and lack of judgement of children, proposing, "Talking with children about race from an early age may not only derail embarrassing questions, but may, more importantly, serve to increase children's comfort when interacting with people from different racial and ethnic groups – and increase the comfort of those they are interacting with too." In our increasingly multi-cultural society, equipping children with the skills to talk about race in a curious way feels quite important. Schools play a critical role in the development of this literacy and yet the education system itself, in common with many structures of society, is not necessarily a good role model in this space. "Race and racism in English secondary schools" published by Runnymede in 2020, states in their study:

> Several respondents argued that the cultivation of racial literacy should be seen as an ongoing process of learning and unlearning. Rather than

as a tick-box "skill" that one might acquire and retain with little effort, teachers should understand racial literacy as a constant journey, and they should be given the time, support and resources to pursue that journey. It should be part of continued professional development within schools.

With headteachers struggling to staff basic posts and mend the leaky roof, this is unlikely to be seen as a priority.

One of the most powerful exercises in racial identity in young people ever conducted was that of the Clark Doll's Test. This was a psychological experiment devised by Kenneth and Mamie Clark in the 1940s in the US. This may seem a long time ago, but this experiment has been repeated several times and the results are consistent. The Clarks found that young black children showed a preference for white dolls, suggesting even at this very early age, they had formed a negative self-identity. The original video is still available to view on YouTube (Clark and Clark, 1947). I have watched the video in many rooms and witnessed adults reduced to tears as young black children identify black dolls as naughty and ugly, with the final twist: the last question about which doll looks like them. The look of confusion and pain as they point to the black doll will stay with many viewers. Try telling those young children the world is colour-blind. In the northern hemisphere, the concept of systemic racial inferiority is well ingrained in our three- and four-year-olds.

For the women I interviewed, there were several examples of colour-blindness which did not feel helpful, as it limited the opportunity for them to reach the ethnic identification stage.

More active reflection, dialogue and celebration of difference allows greater growth and should be encouraged early in life.

Making Yourself Very Small

Nilima shared: "I think you take it on board that there is something wrong with you and that there is something wrong with the way you look, because you are different." I have previously explored in terms of social psychology that, as we grow up, we are desperate to be in the in-group, forming our social identity, in part by comparison. We can conclude with some confidence that an early sense of there being something wrong with you will impact negatively on self-confidence and self-esteem.

Earlier in this book, we explored the process of the creation of self-identity. We know low self-esteem leads to low confidence, which, in turn, often results in not speaking up, not taking risks and children of colour potentially missing out on life-affirming experiences because of fear; fear of rejection, fear of humiliation, fear of failure or a deep, irrational fear that comes from years of feeling not good enough.

Talia literally talked of feeling silenced: "I started to think I better keep quiet about anything to do with me; And that was easy because you can talk about yourself in any way, and I denied who I was." The cost of fitting in is draining and masking, whether conscious or unconscious, requires emotional labour.

For me personally, my early memories are that I just wanted to fit in and so I would avoid anything that drew attention. I would try and make myself small. I would also try and be helpful and accommodating. I can think of so many little examples, from letting my friend Joanne have my gloves as she was sledging, only to be scolded at home because they got holes in them, to going on my first school trip and buying presents for friends and not my family. I still have a strong "people pleaser" driver to this day, which does not always serve me well.

Virginia described a similar memory of her early teens saying she would try and be accepted: "There was a sense of don't draw attention to yourself; don't do anything that makes you stand out; just fit in." This led her to reflect that she probably did not have as much fun as she should have had!

Sadia clearly stated: "Othering has given me real self-confidence issues." She describes a discomfort about her difference at primary school affecting her poise and confidence to speak.

Lorella who has rarely been with a majority of black people, either in child-hood or adulthood, described the persistent nature of her reaction: "It's almost like muscle memory, trying to shrink and be on the periphery and trying not to be either the angry black woman or somebody to be feared and viewed with suspicion." She described the emotional effort of constantly scanning, judging whether you are going to be safe in new environments. If you are not different in some way, it is almost impossible to understand this pervasive, underlying anxiety. LGBTQ friends and colleagues describe a very similar fear of going into bars, for example, question-ing whether they will be abused for showing affection.

The drive for Others or for migrants to assimilate is created by strong social pressure. Those with power lay dichotomous responsibility at the feet of migrants, wanting both the exotic difference in things like food and culture, while also laying down very clear expectations of what being "one of us" means. The word "assim-ilation" feels negative to me, but maybe that is because I watched too much *Star Trek* as a child and it reminds me of the Borg, the cyber-connected hive, known as the "Collective". The collective appropriated the technology and resources of other galactic species though a process of assimilation. When I call for collective action, this is most certainly not what I mean.

The Impact of Racism and Micro-aggressions

I have already mentioned Nilima's encounter with the National Front. My last expe-rience of racism in Lancaster was as a 17-year-old. I was walking through town with my sister and a group of boys shouted "Paki" and threw an orange, which hit me full on in the arm and did actually really hurt. A few onlookers showed concern. One elderly gentleman actually came over and asked if we were okay. I had long since given up correcting the fact that technically I couldn't be a "Paki", because my family were from India not Pakistan. I remember being both shocked and slightly bemused. Why an orange? Even in those days oranges were relatively expensive as a fruit.

"Sticks and stones will break my bones, but names will never hurt me" dates back, it is thought, to the 19th century as a rhyme.

It isn't true.

We know being abused, ridiculed or belittled verbally can have lasting effects on self-confidence and self-esteem. Even in early childhood, there is a sense of sadness, confusion and hurt from the name calling. Virginia described her upset when a boy she was friendly with called her a "chocolate drop". In hearing her tell this story, it felt like it was the betrayal of this coming from a friend that made it really sting. Again, that deep sense of unfairness surfaces.

We explored earlier the connection between the trauma of racist experiences and physical health and indeed the possibility that our very genetic makeup can be altered through events.

We know racism also impacts negatively on mental health. Nandi, Luthra and Benzeval (2020) found that experiencing "ethnic and racial harassment" was strongly linked to psychological distress as measured by the General Health Questionnaire. This can have negative impacts in many aspects of life, relationships and the workplace. There is evidence, however, that those who strongly identify or are embedded within an ethnic identity are less likely to be impacted negatively. In other words, racist experiences have a less detrimental impact on mental wellbeing, when experienced in the context of a strong association to a culture, even if that is not the dominant culture. It appears this sense of belonging offers a protective effect.

They also, interestingly, found that those born in the UK had a stronger distress response than first generation immigrants. This is somewhat surprising, but I wonder if the expectations of first and second generations are different. As someone born in this country, I expect to be valued in society and treated fairly. Perhaps first-generation immigrants had lower expectations and a greater belief that they will be subject to racial harassment. The fact that experiencing racism impacts more on those born in this country, with respect to harm to mental wellbeing, poses a significant challenge to society in terms of how we move to genuine equality.

Even into adulthood, careless comments can cause hurt. Talia described working in her forties in a development programme with three other facilitators. She arrived in a Shalwar Kameez, a traditional South Asian outfit, and one of the other facilitators said "Oh, I didn't know we were dressing up." A thoughtless comment, but one that arguably dismissed and diminished Talia's identity. I myself still remember an experience in my early thirties where I was asked if I would be photographed for some posters for a part of the public sector by my friend, who was in a marketing and engagement role. In the end she told me my photograph was not used because her manager said I did not look "ethnic" enough. Not only did I have to experience insidious discrimination in my working life, but a white middle-class woman got to decide I wasn't brown, or different, enough. With hindsight she probably wanted someone who wore a Hijab or who had a clearer physical identity related to a different race or religion. This is yet another example, however, of where lack of thought and clumsy language can cause hurt.

Much of the work I do in the inclusion space is aimed at exposing and challenging assumptions. Often individuals are so keen to show their cultural awareness that they jump in without checking the facts. In my early twenties, one of my friends who was half Jamaican and half Irish looked much like me. She described a situation where she started a new job and had an induction with a director, who attempted to regale her with how much he knew about and respected Indian culture. Needless to say, she did not seek him out in the rest of her employment there. I have often wondered whether his mistake was ever brought to his attention.

Lorella described an incident where because she is black of Afro-Caribbean descent, a colleague commented on how she could associate with a new member of staff who was of Nigerian descent. Culturally they are quite different, but the colleague failed to see beyond the immediate physical similarity.

Through my interviews, I became aware that the 1970s music group Boney M. have a lot to answer for. The 1978 song "Brown Girl in the Ring" was mentioned by several interviewees as a point in the playground or even school assembly when they were singled out and put in the middle of the ring. This will rarely have been done with malicious intent, but even if the memory was that, at the time, we did not feel significantly distressed, Lorella, Nilima and myself, can look back with considerable discomfort. Lorella stated: "Only in retrospect do I realise that probably is not okay. But when you are six or seven, you don't understand and I suppose it was normalised." Lorella also shared an experience much later in life, when she distanced a friend because she was offended when Lorella expressed her preference that she did not constantly touch her son's hair. Another almost stereotypical micro-aggression, the fascination with Afro hair!

As we transition into adulthood, our sense of confidence and the realisation of difference takes on a different lens. An early experience I remember is being told at the age of 11 by a friend who was very popular, that one boy in my class, David had said: "Rita would be okay if she was white." This was genuinely presented as a pseudo compliment, as if my colour was something I could change, like a new haircut or a trendier pair of jeans.

The fact I still remember this comment into my fifties shows the impact it had in terms of my self-worth, and that impact was, needless to say, not positive.

Suki talked of the impact of her realisation that others see her in a different way and ascribe behaviours and characteristics to her as "painful". This pain was related to the fact people who did not know her would make assumptions and this for her, in some way, denied her identity. The homogenising effect of Othering creates distress, as we all want our individuality to be recognised and for us to be seen. In Zulu culture, we see the open-hearted practice of Sawubona, where humans connect with the words "I see you", the usual response being either "I see you too", or "I am here". The simple acknowledgement of another person's unique being; a precious gift.

Nilima described starting a new school in an area that was not at all diverse, at the age of 12. The teacher introduced her to the class and the majority of the children in the class just started laughing. It may have been her colour. It may have been the fact she had a long, unusual surname. Not many 12-year-olds would be psychologically resourced to deal with that. I cannot imagine how that felt. Actually, I probably can.

The impact of micro-aggressions and discrimination heightened for some as they entered the world of work. Virginia described how she did not feel particularly different as a child but growing up in a very white area, she experienced clear discrimination when applying for summer jobs. She gives an example of where she was told a job had been filled, only to discover that her white friend went in the following day and was given the job. Later she applied for a graduate job in the aviation industry and was told she was the best candidate for the job, but they would not be offering her the role as they were not sure "people would accept you". I suspect employers would be a bit more subtle about this now, but can we really be sure it does not still happen?

Sadia also talks of her first graduate job being in an organisation with little diversity and a lack of psychological safety. She could not work out the rules and what was acceptable and not acceptable. In the end, having spoken out, she was literally removed from the firm. This had an enormously negative impact on her. She shared: "I became a bit of a shell of myself and my confidence had been completely shattered." She then moved organisations in what she called "out of the frying pan, into the fire" with a boss who was an extreme bully. While the ill treatment she reported in this role was not directly related to race, it clearly had a cumulative effect in terms of her self-worth and confidence.

Nilima also spoke of the negative reaction to challenge and "calling out". In this context, by calling out, I am referring to the act of challenging an individual or organisation about negative behaviour and sharing its impact. Nilima noticed in her Master's course that in year one there were numerous people of colour in the cohort and by year three, there were very few non-white students. She herself then started to get poor marks and negative feedback from her tutor. She discussed this with fellow students and compared work and, ultimately, she made a complaint which was upheld. She describes the university reaction, however, which was essentially to brush it under the carpet. Nilima, due to the impact of this stressful situation, never did complete her Master's degree.

There is undoubtedly psychological impact that shapes our current and future responses. Our past experiences influence how we respond to situations. Even Kirsten, who described her experience of being Othered as resilience-building, states: "There were horrible things and the feelings that invokes are still there. I think people forget how easy it is to tap into the feeling once you have experienced it once." She talks of how she sometimes responds to perceived injustice in the workplace with strong emotional feelings she can connect to her past.

Our Parents' Trauma

This is perhaps the hardest section to write as, in immersing myself in the stories of these women and their families, it was hard not to be slightly overwhelmed by the collective pain and angered by the sometimes careless, or sometimes intentional, way in which this was inflicted. I had no realisation as I grew up of the reality of the lives of my parents as first-generation immigrants and, as I spoke to the women I interviewed, there were many common experiences. I could not understand my parents focus on education, on being better than everyone else was, in part, driven by injustices they had experienced. I write this having just watched the BBC Proms 2023 in what felt a very significant moment of progress. A tribute to Lata Mangeshkar, the so called "nightingale of India", beautifully presented by the City of Birmingham Symphony Orchestra and the very talented Muchhal siblings, primarily Palak. It brought back vivid memories of being bored at Preston cinema when my parents took me to watch Hindi or Bollywood films. My sister and I had no interest or understanding and would run around the cinema, much to the annoyance of other cinema goers, I can imagine. My mum's favourite was a film called *Kabhi Kabhie*, and I must confess to tears when Palak sang that song so beautifully that night. Music was important to me growing up. I cannot imagine not having access to the music I love, and I reflected on how hard it must have been to live in a cultural vacuum, disconnected from all that was familiar and comforting.

The world was a lot less connected then. We didn't have streaming and social media and even making calls was expensive and unreliable. My parents learned of their parents' deaths through telegrams. There was no sense of closure, no funeral to attend. Even if they had been able to afford to go, in Hindu culture funerals occur the same day or, at the very latest, the following day, so there would have been no time for my parents to get there. Of course, it was their choice to move, but I wonder if the many that made that choice really knew what awaited them and what they were giving up?

What exacerbated the loneliness and sense of disconnection for those first-generation immigrants was the less than enthusiastic welcome from some.

Talia spoke in an animated manner about her father shouting about the signs on rental properties in his early years in the UK: "no Irish, no blacks, no dogs, no Pakis". He indignantly raged about the fact that the group he belonged to were seen as lower than dogs in his adopted homeland. Talia shared her retrospective view, stating: "That's the level of trauma he carried with him; really this was very apparent in our family life. I didn't know it at the time."

Lorella too, although her mother was not keen to talk about racism, describes conversations with her father, an Afro-Caribbean man, separated from her mother, about the racism he experienced. She valued these conversations which gave her more insight into systemic racism. Lorella talked of how hard her mum worked as a single mother, and the multiple jobs, to give her children a better life and opportunities not afforded to her. Her approach was very much, however, that you are here and you need to integrate. Discussing difference was not seen as helpful or necessary.

My own father, who was a good, principled man, had a quick temper in certain situations. He would often shout in shops, and I remember being confused on occasions. I have a vivid memory of being in a bed shop with my parents when I was around 13 and there was an older, obviously white, salesman and he was talking about the time he spent in India in the military and he was referring to the women in a fairly lewd way. The complete inappropriateness of talking to my dad about what I assume were prostitutes while he was buying a bed for his young teenage daughter feels hard to comprehend. Upon reflection, I am left feeling, no wonder my dad was so quick to anger when there were so many situations in which he was not treated with thought or dignity. This may not have been explicitly about race; the salesman could have been insensitive to others, but it is hard not to interpret it through that lens.

In work, despite his intelligence and knowledge, he never rose above junior management levels. He was overlooked for promotions, in part because he did not fit in. He did not go to the "pub" for drinks on a Friday or play golf. The settings where decisions are often made were not accessible to him. He admirably found ways around this by finding status and recognition in other ways. For many years, he was a Justice of the Peace or magistrate in his adopted town, a visitor for a young offender institute, and he was also Chairman of the Hindu Society of Lancaster and Morecambe. While he never sought positional power or recognition, I can recognise, on reflection, the healing generated for him by the taking on of these roles.

My mother, meanwhile, who was a teacher in India, did not have her qualifications considered as equivalent on arriving in England in the mid-1960s, and the only work she could get was as a sewing machinist. We were well stocked with underwear from a well-known high street brand, but I regret that as a child I never reflected on how hard it must have been for my mum, an educated woman, to go to a factory day in, day out and not have the choices open to her that I later took for granted. I was very proud that decades later in her early sixties she taught Gujarati at the local Further Education College. Being a teacher was her first and last job, and so I felt no sense of deception in writing "teacher" on her death certificate.

Others describe the trauma in complex ways. Can you imagine what it must have been like for a Japanese woman to come to the UK in the post-war years? Miki talked of the downright hostility and the under-current of fear which permeated the family. Not surprising, in some respects, that for long periods of her life, Miki's mother suffered with her mental health.

Nilima shared the racial abuse and actual threats of physical violence her father suffered when running a corner shop in a rural part of the UK. Three young men coming towards you with a broken bottle, in a threatening manner, is not an encounter you are likely to forget in a hurry.

Talia, meanwhile, told of the challenge that her parents' marriage created in terms of cultural clash. A Pakistani family that expected her father to go back and have an arranged marriage, securing a partnership of wealthy families, was scuppered by an inconvenient pregnancy. Her mother, who was from an equally privileged but European background, vowed to bring up the child alone. In the end the two parents did marry, but it was a traumatic start and, even here, racial prejudice played in. At their marriage, the Registrar said to Talia's mother that her father could have four wives and she was "already seven months gone". Hardly the most auspicious start to a life partnership.

She also described that when she went onto university, she used to come back and he would often say: "who do you think you are?". That must have been so incredibly hurtful, but now she sees it was his trauma leaking, as he never realised his dream of going to Oxford and getting a degree. She shared that he was a member of a golf club, had to have a Rolex and a Mercedes, stating: "He showed his success to justify that he was good enough, because he just didn't understand that he was good enough."

Sadia described her parents as very "risk averse", a state which could be related to the insecurities of being first generation immigrants. This risk averseness played out unhelpfully in her early adult life when they encouraged her to stay in a job which was harming her psychologically.

For some parents, choosing to live in an area where there were few minority communities led to them having little access to their cultural heritage. It was quite hard in the seventies to buy West Indian food in parts of the UK! It is not surprising, in these circumstances, that gradually, the association with one's heritage diminishes.

We know that first generation immigrant parents can have a negative impact on the mental wellbeing of children. This is normally unintentional, but can cause problems and reduce the feelings of belonging in young people born into a different culture. Parents can follow cultural norms which mean they can be controlling, limit autonomy and over-stress academic and financial achievements. They can get stuck living in a vacuum of how their birth countries were when they left. It is entirely understandable that when faced with losing so much, they cling desperately to their own social constructs of what is right and how to parent. Our parents were not perfect, but the more we reflect on their experiences, the more we can look back with understanding, acceptance and gratitude.

In being in conversation with the women, I felt a palpable sense of the headwinds that our parents would have experienced. The extra effort, the opportunities not afforded to them, the micro-aggressions whittling away at one's sense of self-worth. There was no psychological support offer, in those days, to help them process how they were feeling and to guide them with compassion.

Only now, with the benefit of knowledge I did not possess as a child, do I feel the need to recognise and honour the courage and resilience of our parents' generation, my own parents included.

The Legacy of Shame

Shame was a word that was mentioned numerous times in the interviews. My own interest in shame came through reading the work of Brené Brown. Her 2010 book, *The Gifts of Imperfection*, came to me at a point in my life where I needed it. I recall reading it as I caught a train to Heathrow in 2016 to join a study trip to the Veteran's Association in Minneapolis; a trip which was no longer relevant as my career working at executive level in the National Health Service (NHS) had just come to a rather abrupt end.

I had been successful in a career in the NHS and worked in four board level roles. In 2015, I was seconded out of a Chief Officer role to lead a system-level transformation programme across nine organisations. Interestingly when I took it, a number of people, including people in the then Department of Health, told me it was a "poisoned chalice", which turned out to be prophetic, as I was not given a chance to succeed in this endeavour. I had accountability, but no authority or resources and I made many mistakes, one of which was being naïve about the actions of others. I do not believe my colour was a significant factor in this scenario, but my sense and conversations with others indicated that gender definitely was. Some male colleagues did not easily accept my leadership and acted to ensure the programme failed, including initiating the involvement of junior ministers, as they did not believe it would deliver. I ended up potentially being sidelined and utterly exhausted, but thankfully I had enough strength left to take control and choose to walk away, with the support of my family. This was not the life I, or indeed, we wanted to live and ultimately I was proud of how I exited.

This is not the place for a critique of leadership and culture in the English National Health Service. Others have directed their talent to that endeavour. I can say that before I left, my working life felt more and more like a scene in *Alice in Wonderland* every day, with increasingly non-sensical interactions.

Reading Brené's book was the start of a healing process for me personally, and a marker of the transition in my life to coach, facilitator and someone who thinks more deeply about human and world systems. I am still working on the self-kindness, but I can honestly say, her work remains one of the founding underpinnings of my practice and when I am feeling fragile I often go back to it.

Brené talks of the need for wholeheartedness and self-compassion. Her premise is that one of the key things that gets in the way of this is the concept she labels as shame. This shame makes us lose our perspective and fail to believe anything positive about ourselves; it leads us to a place of self-loathing. Her response to moments of shame is to connect intentionally to those within her circle of trust. She characterises shame in the following way: "Shame hates it when we reach out and tell our story, It hates having words wrapped around it-it can't survive being shared. Shame loves secrecy."

Brené too, therefore, appears to be suggesting that the key to reducing the shame which may be created through an experience of Othering is to engage in dialogue; in generative conversation with those we can trust to hear and honour our story.

The origins of shame start in childhood, and it is likely negative experiences of ethnic identification could exacerbate feelings of shame in people of colour. It is also related to my findings that young people of colour are inclined to make themselves small. Brandt (2021) states:

> You are afraid of looking stupid or saying the wrong thing, so you don't try new things and don't speak up. You avoid being the centre of attention and wish you could shrink into the walls. Shame makes you feel like you can't be your true self and that your true self is inadequate.

Kaufman (2004) shares in his book *The Psychology of Shame*: "In the context of normal development, shame is the source of low self-esteem, diminished self-concept and deficient body-image." He argues that the experience of shame leads to low levels of security and confidence. He also explicitly addresses the potential for enhanced levels of shame linked to a minority cultural identity.

I increasingly feel this could be linked to the hyper-vigilance and visceral response to micro-aggressions. Of course, I am not saying all women of colour are crippled with feelings of shame. It could be hypothesised, however, that the disadvantage experienced by them makes this more likely than in white communities, when other factors such as education, wealth and health are taken into account.

The shame described in the interviews was complex and multi-faceted. The desire to fit in is so strong that in some cases, interviewees expressed embarrassment about their identity and a desire to disassociate from family. This can have impact later in life, with Talia describing her subsequent "guilt trip" when she reflects on her childhood thoughts and behaviour. I can connect with that sense of guilt as there were certainly times, if I am honest, when I was embarrassed about my identity and my name. I had a very long, difficult to pronounce, surname, "Upadhyay", and there were times I longed for a world where I had my mum's maiden name, "Mehta".

One of my earliest memories in terms of the focal point for my excruciating embarrassment was my hair. My mum, in traditional Indian style, oiled my hair and put it in a complicated style every day. The hair was pulled tight into two pigtails, which were then plaited and tied back around, then tied with big ribbons. So, I effectively had two plaited rings, which resembled black pretzels. It looked quite cute when I was three; less so at nine. I remember being acutely aware of how different my hair was compared to those around me. I begged my mother at the age of ten to take me to have my hair cut, to which she thankfully conceded. The plaited pigtails were gone and I had one less thing that caused me to be a subject of difference and ridicule. Virginia, too, described her hair as a source of difference and potential shame. She shared that her hair was long in her younger years and her parents encouraged her not to wear it down because it looked somewhat wild, the message being that it would make her look "unruly".

Miki named shame as something she was not able to fully understand, but could intuitively feel as a child. She shared: "I just knew it; there was something to be ashamed of." She felt this was intensified by the lack of connection to any one community she and her sister experienced. There was no one like her in her life for her to self-reference against.

Sadia talked of the vulnerability of the teenage years, sharing: "when you are already hypersensitive to things and actually feeling that you don't fit in, it can really exacerbate negative situations". She described situations where she did not volunteer for activities at school and a heightened sense of distress when things did not go well.

We can see how shame can be life-limiting and there is evidence that shame related to negative self-evaluation can elicit a stress response. Lewis and Ramsay (2002) studied stress responses in four-year-olds and they discovered that there were two differing types of stress reactions to embarrassing situations. Shame-related reactions, particularly linked to poor self-image, resulted in greater levels of cortisol, a stress hormone, being released.

There is a link to the concept of "imposter syndrome", which was originally coined by Clance and Imes in 1978. In my coaching practice, I would estimate around one in three clients mention imposter syndrome as an issue for them. I have to confess, while many of the things I hear feel very real and impactful, it does feel like imposter syndrome is a phenomenon that has become too easily cited; too common in our parlance and often used inappropriately. Imposter syndrome relates to feelings of success not being deserved or being accidently achieved and a sense one will be found out or exposed as not capable. There is some evidence that this is more prevalent in women of colour. Raypole (2021) argues that it is more prevalent in women of colour who are less represented in professional environments. She also cites evidence that the existence of imposter syndrome leads to higher levels of anxiety and depression.

It feels like shame is an unwelcome bedfellow, a consequence of our choice to live in an ego-centric paradigm. In the supposed, difficult to evidence words of Carl Jung, however, "shame is a soul-eating emotion". He may or may not have said this, but it rings true with what else we know.

The need to practice self-compassion and actively challenge our shame is paramount if we are to live with joy and peace. The good news is we can, in part, silence the monster by shining the light on it. This is work I would encourage everyone with even a hint of self-loathing to do.

The Importance of Shade

Agarwal (2020) has a subheading in her book on unconscious bias, "Fair and Lovely", which interestingly is the name of a cream produced by Hindustan Unilever. Here, she talks of the adoption of western standards of beauty. She shares a story I can absolutely relate to, as I suspect many women of South Asian origin can. I distinctly remember in the summer of 1976, a blisteringly hot season, my mother shouting at me to come in from the garden, not because I might burn or get dehydrated, but because I would get too black or dark. I personally found the prevalence of bleaching creams when I first went to India deeply disturbing; even at the age of 11 I knew there was something instinctively wrong about this.

"Colourism" is not formally adopted as a word, but was thought to be coined by the writer Alice Walker in her book *In Search of Our Mother's Gardens* in 2005. She described it as "prejudicial or preferential treatment of same-race people based solely on their colour".

Numerous reviews of high-end fashion magazines and other media sources show a preference for light-skinned subjects. It is so endemic we rarely stop to think about it.

The writer Candice Braithwaite wrote in *The Guardian* newspaper on 27 February 2021 that it is time to face up to colourism. This is a phenomenon that is ingrained in society and she points out: "It comes from within the community as well as without, and is an issue across many races, including mine." She describes growing up in Brixton, a multicultural part of London, and the fact for her colourism was more of an issue than racism. She shares that for her "the penny dropped" when a black boy told her she was too "dark and ugly" to be pursued in a game of kiss chase. She also described being overlooked to present programmes as most black presenters on television, at the time of writing, still tend to be lighter skinned.

As well as facing racism, women of colour also, therefore, have to contend with colourism and the injustices that can lead to. Braithwaite unsurprisingly states: "I am personally pretty exhausted." Colourism may be a consequence of colonial history, but it is perpetuated by communities of the global majority. There is such irony in the fact that many people pursue tans to make them darker, whilst maintaining the myth of darkness as somehow less.

Coming back to the women I interviewed, the differential experience of siblings based on colour was very evident in the research findings. Virginia described that she had a sister who was darker and a brother who was much lighter who could pass for white. In contrast her other brother looked more Afro-Caribbean. She recounted how the teachers at school treated him very differently. She revealed that the teacher always appeared to assume the worst, attributing negative characteristics to this darker brother, often with no supporting evidence. Virginia described a shocking story of the teacher locking him in a cupboard. Beyond a micro-aggression, I would argue that to be downright abuse.

Talia, who is of dual heritage, talked of her sisters being darker and having very different life experiences, with more overt racism. The eldest, who she said was quite hairy, was unkindly called a monkey in school and her younger sister was regularly called a "Paki".

Kirsten, who is also of mixed heritage, shared that she felt she suffered from less evident racism in her younger years, potentially because of her lighter skin colour.

Much closer to home, I experience this with my own daughters. My eldest is fairer and was often mistaken for being of Mediterranean origin. My youngest is darker and looks more obviously Asian. She has experienced more examples of microaggressions, with the usual questions like "Where are you really from?" Ironically, she faced verbal abuse in both directions, with so called friends of Asian origin calling her a "coconut", a phrase coined to mean brown on the outside and white in the middle. Not that surprising as she has a white father. Thinking about this still makes me really angry, but it also leaves me curious. What made them think that was acceptable? Later in the book, you will read of the complex norms around language in modern South Africa, as associated with colour.

Again, this shows the complexity of issues around race. While racism for some is still clearly linked to normative whiteness, the ability to discriminate or inflict hurt based on race is not limited to white communities. That said, let me be clear.

I do not believe in the concept of reverse racism as a construct and I condemn the response to the "Black Lives Matters" movement which manipulated the language to "All Lives Matter". Denying history and systemic injustice is unhelpful, dismissive and cynical, and does not help in the fight to achieve inclusive communities.

All difference can make children a target, but there is something very obvious about colour as opposed to other difference, for example neuro-divergence, which can remain unseen for some time. Going back to the science, we know our unconscious brain responds from an early age to different colour with fear and cautiousness. We could hypothesise that the darker the skin, the greater the automatic fear response.

We need to be far more intentional in teaching our children about the beauty of black skin. When walking in the park, I once saw a white family with two young children, one of which was holding intently onto a very black doll. It made me smile and I found myself wondering what the impact would be if every child was given a black doll and told it was something to treasure.

Brothers and Sons

Although this book is aimed at exploring the female experience, and I cannot relate personally as I had no brothers and have two lovely daughters, a theme that did emerge was the differential, and often more violent or visceral experience of men of colour in the lives of the interviewees.

Lorella, who has two teenage mixed-race sons and lives in an affluent part of London, described her unease when they go out in casual clothes, in particular in "hoodies". Her fear is well founded, with young black men three times more likely to be killed in London than the general population and much more likely to be stopped and searched by the Metropolitan Police. We all worry to some extent as our children turn into adults and start to spend more time away from us. I can only imagine the added burden of worrying about your child being a victim of violence every time they leave the house.

For some, ironically, a focus on the wellbeing of their sons may not always have been paramount. Due to her own experiences related to gender in her family, Suki described how she was so supportive of her daughters, focusing substantial energy on ensuring they felt they could achieve anything. She reflected that in doing this she may have inadvertently given less of her attention to her son, and she actively rebalanced this when her children were young adults. She stated that she realised: "I also have a young man who needs that level of support."

As an Asian young man, Suki's son will be subject to discrimination, but the worst impact at a societal level is still experienced by black men. Goff et al. (2014) stated in a publication for the American Psychological Association that "We find converging evidence that Black boys are seen as older and less innocent and that they prompt a less essential conception of childhood than do their White same-age peers." They talked of the dehumanising that routinely occurs and commented on the subsequent dangers of this inter-group difference in perception.

I have already shared Virginia's brother's negative experience in school, being locked in a cupboard by a teacher. A 2020 report by the YMCA called "Young and Black" found that 95 per cent of black British people have witnessed racist language in schools, more than half of males said they heard racist language in schools "all of the time", a figure which was only 4 per cent for girls. It does appear, therefore, that young males of colour have a potentially very different experience to females. Interestingly and depressingly, for both sexes, in this report it was cited that teacher perceptions based on race were seen as the biggest barrier to academic attainment.

Black children are also disproportionately likely to be excluded from school, further harming their life chances. In my view, this is caused by the adultification of black young people and the fact they are, therefore, perceived to be less innocent and vulnerable. We have already explored evidence for this for black girls, but there is equally evidence of this effect for boys.

The report also investigated young black people's views of the police: 64 per cent of people surveyed said they worried about being treated fairly by the police and 55 per cent worried about being falsely accused of a crime.

It seems unlikely that this fear would not impact in a way that is potentially harmful.

Evaristo (2019) creates the character Omafe, a woman of Nigerian descent, whose husband goes back to Nigeria and takes a second wife, leaving her in London with two sons. The book captures her despair when they get caught up in crime, and she bemoans that she will be visiting their graves or engaging in weekly visits to the local prison. Drastic measures then follow as she tells them they are going on holiday to Nigeria and then unbeknown to them, having taken out a loan, enrols them in a strict Nigerian boarding school. The act of a mother desperate to keep her boys safe.

Lewis-Oduntan (2020) writes of the reality of being a Black British mum bringing up sons. She shares she was not surprised by George Floyd's death because, for her, young black people being killed is normalised and something she chooses not to focus on, as a conscious coping strategy. She states it is "something completely different to know that one day you'll have to try and explain to your child that they've been operating from a disadvantaged position since the moment they took their first breath". A heartbreaking position for any mother to be in.

If we can shift the dial in terms of creating fairer societies, countless woman will not have to have that conversation with their sons. That feels like a goal worth aiming for.

In the Workplace

In the world of work, intersectionality means women of colour often face greater challenges.

It is hard enough being a woman in the modern workplace, let alone a woman who must deal with racial stereotypes. We know that as women age, they can be faced with pressures and perceptions that stack the odds up further against them. Ryan (2023) in her wonderfully titled book *Revolting Women* evidences this, talking about the value placed on youth and citing numerous examples of how women over the age of 50 were sidelined, ignored and denigrated. Harris et al. (2017) conducted a meta-analysis of studies, 43 in total, and concluded that with ageism, which affects the young and older outliers in organisations, older people are likely to be viewed as "less trainable, flexible, and efficient, and as lacking necessary physical capabilities and technological proficiency". Ouch!

For women, we can add the uncomfortable fact that looks still matter and women are expected to age well to be seen as relevant and valuable in the workplace. Ryan (2023) introduces the controversial concept of "erotic capital". How you look as a woman is important, however senior you are, and she describes the extensive lengths some of the women she interviewed went to in order to maintain a fit and youthful appearance. In my experience, the same pressure is not put on men. Rather, it appears, the pressure is put on women by social constructs created by men to hold on to old power and to comply with the perceived truth. The sad truth, also, is women often are the perpetuators of this, being the ones who tell younger counterparts they need to dress differently or wear more make up. When the common perception is still there that there needs to be one token woman in the team, women often undermine more ambitious attempts at greater equality by competing with each other. Kiner (2020) discusses this in a Harvard Business Review paper and talks of female rivalry. She shares her view that: "Women unconsciously absorb beliefs about their rightful place, and those messages show up in how women judge each other. That can lead women to mistreat, underestimate, and distance themselves from other women in order to increase their power and standing among men." She also states that both women and men judge women more harshly than men in the workplace. Is it time for women to be more reflective on our behaviours and ask ourselves honestly, are we colluding to maintain the current paradigm? In believing the "one seat at the table" myth, are we falling into the trap of the scarcity mindset? Do we need to rise?

Perhaps we need to heed the words of Maya Angelou (1978) in her wonderful, hypnotic poem, "Still I Rise". Women are powerful; they are life givers; they are goddesses. In her words, she unapologetically invites readers to question their limiting assumptions about the power and sheer force of feminine energy.

In parallel to the power imbalance which surrounds the construct of race, in her book Ryan (2023) goes on to discuss the history in relation to gender, reminding us that even in ancient Greek times the female body was somehow less; viewed as a problem, as capricious and weak. More recently, history shows when we were needed in the workplace, for example, in World War II, women were accepted, but post-war, in the 1950s, there was a move back when the men came home. The common narrative was of the idealised woman as homemaker, popping on her make up in the early evening to welcome her husband home from work with a gin and tonic, dinner ready to serve. There is undoubtedly a better balance, but how many of our friends and acquaintances would describe women still doing most of the domestic duties? There are, of course, notable exceptions. In my interviews, Talia described that she was the main earner, but her partner did do most of the shopping, cleaning and cooking. Indeed, Talia described herself as a terrible cook!

Returning to the "erotic capital" cited by Ryan, some of the women I interviewed described sexual advances in the workplace, the unspoken belief being you may be good at your job, but ultimately, your worth was measured through the lens of sexualisation. Duske (2016), an American psychotherapist, reflected on female sexualisation, stating: "We are bombarded with hypersexualized images of females, so much so that most of us don't even notice them. They are all around us like the air we breathe; messages so blatant, they become invisible, encouraging the normalization of female objectification." As a woman of colour herself, Duske also shared that her blonde step-sister told her she was "the colour of poop", a comment unlikely to make her feel positive about herself.

I remember, as a very senior executive in the health service in my thirties and forties, it was very common for me to go to a meeting with a male colleague and receive unsolicited complimentary comments about my clothes or appearance. I am sure most of those men would never comment on how sharp a male colleague's suit looked! Virginia talked of the fact she dressed very conservatively as she was conscious of the stereotype of a black woman as more sexually available. She shared: "I was a full-figured black woman; I would get lots of attention and people would make very sexualised approaches." An additional consideration I am sure she could have done without in a demanding role, and she described how she tried to redirect attention to her "intellect and conscientiousness".

The women I interviewed have had mixed experiences at their place of work, as one would expect. I cannot recall my exact feelings as I started my first job in 1990 in Public Health, but I do remember embarking naively into the world of meaningful employment with the assumption that it would all be good and there would be no negative experiences. What ignorance!

For some of the women, such as Suki, there was always some tension between ambition in work and the expectations with respect to caring and family duties. For a few individuals, there was a lesser expectation in terms of level of ambition, despite a focus in some communities on the importance of education. When I was growing up, sadly, a good education was still often seen as an enabler not to a good job, but to a good husband.

For others, such as Virginia, entering the workplace was an experience that brought systemic discrimination sharply into focus. She described earlier in this chapter how she was not initially offered a role because the view was she may not be "accepted". To know that you are well qualified for a job, but literally your face does not fit, must have been a galling experience.

She told of applying for a job, at a senior level, with a prestigious engineering company, and having seven interviews in total, stating: "I had to go through extra layers and jump through more hoops."

She went on to work for a global technology conglomerate and described an ultimately fulfilling career. There were several examples of micro-aggressions, however, as she travelled the world in her Human Resources role. A gentle but assertive black woman was not often seen in many of the boardrooms she inhabited, and the people she worked with often fell into the patterns of making assumptions about her. These assumptions varied but included assuming she was more junior, assuming she was there to tick a diversity box or assuming she would take on the persona of the angry black woman.

Woo (2000) found both systemic and individual discrimination exists for women in the workplace. Sometimes it is manifest. Other times it lies below the surface, with often hidden dynamics at play. She argues, however, it is real and can have a detrimental effect on women's career prospects. She uses the phrase "glass ceiling", a term which has become common parlance. She studied women from many non-dominant cultural and ethnic backgrounds and found the experience of systemic disadvantage remarkably similar across differing groups.

If this is to be believed, the idea drummed into all of us by our parents, that we needed to study and work harder to be successful, appears to be true. Kinouani (2021) shares she too grew up in a household where you had to be "Twice as good as everyone else and certainly twice as good as your white equivalent to simply be deemed good enough to stand underneath them."

Sadia talked of starting her working life in marketing, which was not at all diverse at the time, and she had consecutive poor experiences in her first two substantive roles, where she was treated insensitively and did not feel psychologically safe or that she fitted in. We all face difficulties in work, but for her, the layering of this with experience of being Othered added to the harm. She stated: "At the time, you come from a situation where you have never felt good enough and you just think; oh, it must be me." She described low confidence and a sense of disempowerment, which she only overcame when she then had an incredibly supportive manager who believed in her and encouraged her to progress. Women supporting other women was also an emergent theme from my enquiry. I, myself, had a formidable but very supportive director in my first job. This helped to increase my confidence and propel my early career.

Lorella worked in several sectors, but stated that in all, she experienced a sense of wariness and a need to scan for safety. In many rooms, she was the only black woman, and this could play out in terms of her being an oddity or seen as somehow exotic. She also described that later in her career, she noticed a tendency for her ideas to be ignored; met with what she called a "lukewarm" response, but then subsequently recycled by others, often to her surprise. How many times have we, as women, said something in a meeting, only to hear a positive response, when a man repeats the same point two minutes later? Women are often ignored in the workplace. For a woman of colour, this is often compounded, as white women are just as capable as men at initiating micro-aggressions. Lorella described the tension of balancing the need to have her work and ideas recognised with the risk of her being seen as over-assertive. She also described the positive feelings when she finally came to a job role where she was interviewed by two black women. Her anxiety was reduced by "somebody who looked like me, facing me".

Kirsten worked in professional services and described in her early career the real pressure to fit in and act in line with the dominant culture, which was largely male, task-orientated and where communication tended to be banter-based rather than truly connecting. She states things are now much improved, but there are pockets where old power prevails.

Our conditioning leads us to the assumption that the most senior person in the room must be white. Time and time again this assumption plays out. I remember when I was a Chief Officer of an NHS organisation, technically in charge of a budget of £240m, one of the older general practitioners in a meeting assumed I was there to take the notes. He did at least have the decency to look slightly embarrassed when I was introduced as the Chief Officer!

For some, such as Miki, work was an escape and challenging family dynamics did not hold her back from an impressive and far-ranging career. She too, however, describes that sometimes she went to present to international groups and some men did not identify her as the presenter and looked somewhat surprised when she took the platform.

Talia had an unusual career, starting in acting and then transitioning to use that skill to support leadership development, as well as coaching. She works with many organisations and is skilled at improvisation. She described an organisation for which she is an associate and said that, as a woman of a certain age, she felt invisible and not valued. Again, this indicates that somehow youth is valued disproportionately, ignoring the wisdom acquired over many years.

Interestingly, the views on and about leadership from the women I interviewed were shaped by their personal experience. Suki shared that she never considered herself as a leader, as in her family, leaders were white, middle-aged men who wielded positional power. She said that she didn't associate leadership with selflessness and so never attributed the title of leader to herself, even as she became more senior in her roles. She also described how her upbringing led her not to challenge male bosses, even when she disagreed with the course of action. She stated: "I would just do it, as I didn't think as a female, I could challenge. This is a man telling me what to do; I will do it out of respect." It took her some time to overcome this and be comfortable to challenge. Believing an older man might be wrong and she might be right took considerable self-work.

The need for organisations to be more inclusive and foster belonging is imperative if women of colour are to achieve parity. Women's experience is less positive on average when we look at inclusive practice and experience in organisations. A 2024 report by PWC found statistically lower scores for women compared to men on four dimensions: overall workplace inclusion, belonging, fairness and inclusive decision making. They conclude: "Inclusion at work is empowering and beneficial for all, but especially so for women. A workplace where women feel that they belong, are included in decision-making, and are treated fairly and equitably is a workplace where women can thrive." This makes moral sense, but it also makes business sense, as women with a high inclusion score perform better and are more likely to be positive about their employer.

All the women I interviewed discussed the fact they were somehow, as women of colour, placed in a position where they felt they had to advocate for others and be ambassadors for equality and inclusion. This placed an additional burden in some cases; a sense you cannot just focus on doing your job well. For others, that focus on inclusion became an important part of their identity in the workplace and creating a sense of belonging and psychological safety was identified by some, such as Suki, as something to be proud of.

We may assume that the trajectory is one of improvement, however, with the decline of diversity initiatives, many of the supportive mechanisms that women could access have been removed.

In addition, there is increasing evidence that post the 2020 pandemic, women of colour have been disproportionately and negatively affected. Cox (2023) cites that the reduction in organisational energy focussed on inclusion, together with the fact we know women of colour were more likely to lose jobs in and after the pandemic have led to significant consequences, stating: "This confluence has left women of colour at a particular disadvantage, and in their quest to advance in the workforce and boost their earnings, they may now face an even steeper climb than before." She also cites evidence that women of colour are more likely to leave the workplace due to issues such as childcare. This pattern is deeply worrying and will require active intervention if it is to be addressed. Yet, as the post George Floyd flurry around inclusion becomes old news in many organisations, I worry about where the activism to address this is coming from.

Work forms an important part of our identity and all the women have made, and I am sure will continue to make, significant contributions in their chosen fields. The fact they have had to overcome dual barriers around gender and race makes this all the more admirable.

Shirley Chisholm, the first black woman to be voted to the American Congress, offered this challenge in a 1972 speech:

> Will women dare in numbers sufficient to have an effect on their own attitude towards themselves and thus change the basic attitudes of males and the general society? Women will have to brave the social sanctions in great numbers in order to free themselves from the sexual, psychological, and emotional stereotyping that plagues us. It is not feminine egoism to say that the future of mankind may very well be ours to determine, it is simply a plain fact.

From hearing the courage and determination shown by my interviewees, I feel we can rise to that collective task.

Finding Our Place

We come to the last section of the thematic analysis and I am left feeling that much of the experience I have shared has been negative. This last section, in "Finding Our Place" is unashamedly a celebration. A celebration of the women I interviewed and all the women with parallel stories, who have had similar experiences. In overcoming adversity and focussing on growth and learning, my appreciation is of their resilience, agency and wisdom.

Suki described where she has got to with such power and simplicity: "I am so proud of me as a woman. I am so proud of me as a mom. I'm proud of me as a female and proud of me as a daughter in law. I'm proud of me in the role that I did and everything that I do. And that's very difficult for me to say. And I don't think I would have said that a few years ago. So it's not an easy journey of unravelling in terms of the business of accepting your who you are.

Yes, I am there now, yes."

All of the women I interviewed now engage in some way in work around anti-racism. Many described the need for them to get comfortable in their own identity before being able to engage in this work in a way which was psychologically safe for them. The women talked of this almost as a calling and something they needed to do, feeling they had a role and active part to play in increasing understanding. Sadia stated: "it made me realise the importance of embracing my identity, because actually if you retreat into that and you are not comfortable with it, then that's not helping the cause. That's not helping people to get comfortable with it and understand difference." She now talks of her ambition to further develop coaching and mentoring offers for people from under-represented communities. She noted the lack of diversity in the coaching community, even in a multi-cultural city like London. She is now one of the individuals pioneering different coach training and offers, together with the likes of Salma Shah, who you will hear from later. She made a very intentional decision that she wanted to shift and focus on supporting people, rather than progressing hierarchically in a way that meant she spent most of her time in boards and committee meetings.

The acceptance and celebration of difference is not always an easy journey and many of the women describe it in relation to a life journey and significant events. Suki talks of getting to a place of truly celebrating her identity, stating: "It's taken me 50 years. It's taken me going through the death of both of my parents and a process of really reflecting on who I am as a human being. I think I'd lost myself in marriage and as a mother. I lost what the vision was meant to be." She came to a point in her life where there was space for her to focus on herself.

I can relate to this as it is only after the death of both of my parents that I have been able to focus more fully on my narrative and on this book. That is undoubtedly related to time constraints, but I do wonder if, at the stage in life where you realise you are the oldest generation, this somehow ignites a depth of reflection on our own lives and the legacy we want to leave. Not everyone feels this, but this was common in the women I interviewed; a real focus on impact, and a heightened sense of what we want to spend our time and energy on. There was a real feeling from all the interviewees that they were much more boundaried about what and who they gave their time to. Lorella talked of people who sap her energy, stating: "I remove myself from situations; I just haven't got the bandwidth."

An increased confidence leads to liberating self-permission and more positive self-image, which in many ways counters the fact we don't look as youthful and fit the social norms of beauty any more. Ryan (2023) invites us into this space: "Please join my ranks! Not in decline, or over the hill. Not retiring, but right on the cusp of the next chapter of your life." I, for one, would rather be there than fade into invisibility.

A theme of this book is the need to have courageous, generative conversations. Kirsten describes feeling a deep need to use dialogue as a means of moving forward. She shared: "People are not always conscious, but I think it is important that we help people to recognise the experience of those of us who are different. I think it is really important. So it becomes more positive and there is a bit more compassion and empathy. And curiosity."

Supporting people to lean into the discomfort and gain awareness was mentioned numerous times as a strategy to improve inclusivity in organisations. We will inevitably sometimes get it wrong, but it feels important to try. It is, in my view, impossible to do this challenging work without considerable self-reflection and a level of internal resourcing which allows one to be vulnerable and skilled at holding the anxiety of others.

Lorella talked of how difficult she still finds it as she has years of what she describes as "muscle memory", encouraging her to shrink herself. She does, however, now feel she can be more confident in her own skin. She reported: "I walk in such a way that I am not going to move over. I am taking up space and I deserve to be here. So its small daily acts of rebellion for me."

This is evident in her increased confidence to hold her ground and challenge inappropriate behaviours. This modelling is then impactful in terms of what more junior members of the organisation accept or do not accept, thereby creating a positive ripple in terms of inclusion and belonging in a large organisation. Through holding her ground, she is having a tangible effect on future generations of women.

Talia is much more at peace with her identity and can appreciate her heritage linked to Pakistani culture, while recognising some of the unhelpful power dynamics around gender and sexuality. She no longer feels the need to hide the fact she is mixed race and she has, in recent years, embraced embodied approaches and focussed much more on self-compassion. Some of the self-sabotage and numbing behaviours linked to low confidence and self-esteem have gone and she stands tall, still doing amazing, impactful work.

Miki described a slightly different experience of coming to a point of celebration. She had never focussed on telling her story and indeed revealed that most people would not know her ethnic background. For her the key to unlock self-compassion was faith. She became more engaged in her Buddhist practice and it was this that allowed her to accept and appreciate herself more. She shared: "This is where it has taken me, as in order to see the Buddha in others, you have to believe in yourself." Buddhism has, at its heart, the goal of self-development, and so this feels powerfully congruent. It is still work in progress, but Miki continues to narrow down what she says yes to and focusses on transformational work which gives her joy and a sense of leaving the world a better place. A connection to nature is also a stronger part of her life.

Virginia in finding her place of peace stated that: "There is a sense that I have been on this planet long enough to be comfortable in my own skin." She, too, talked of her knowledge and awareness making her more mindful of other difference, such as disability. She sees herself as an advocate and agent of change, and critically, she felt that self-work was what had helped her to improve her radar and notice injustice in current situations. She has experienced challenges in her life, including significant health challenges, but described a "strong inner core", which has allowed her to stay positive.

Nilima described a sense of self-acceptance and a belief that she knows what her responsibilities and span of control are. She talked of her acceptance that it is not always possible to influence others' views of you and her stance was: "I am happy with who I am; the problem is not with me, but with other people." She, too, shows a confidence which comes with age. She shared: "I don't listen to others' version of the truth; I don't try and be someone else. I think when you are young, you end up doing that to try and be more English or to fit in with the crowd." She believes that the misuse of power by treating Others as inferior remains one of our biggest collective challenges. She is determined to bring up her young daughters to have the confidence and sense of agency to avoid being negatively impacted by this.

The women also described a variety of relationships in their lives and the fact that it is much more acceptable to be in mixed race marriages. I recall my own experience of being welcomed into a fairly typical middle-class English family and reflecting that when my husband and I got engaged, this was a new experience for all. I suspect it was the first time my in-laws had ever visited and stayed with an Indian family. Through the years, a real bond and fondness developed between both sets of parents, who were thrust together by circumstance. We are surrounded by real-life examples of the act of getting to know people as individuals, reducing Othering.

All the women I interviewed were still in employment, either in organisations or self-employed at the time of writing. They described varying situations in terms of relative economic activity and division of labour at home with their significant others. They had, in the main, achieved a balance with which they were content.

In terms of where I am personally, I too am much more intentional with how I choose to spend my time. It does not always work and sometimes I say yes to things I should not, or the challenging work, around race in particular, leads me to the need to consciously resource myself. That said, I feel my own sense of privilege when

I think of the wonderful people I work with and have the honour of calling friends. For me, the career shift in setting up my own business and practice was definitely the right door opening. I am excited and hopeful about what is next.

I end this chapter with renewed appreciation for the women I interviewed and their power, beauty and imperfection.

I also end by sharing their advice to their younger selves.

Miki	*You can get there from here.*
Suki	*Ask lots of questions and be curious. Don't accept just because somebody is different to you, they know better than you. Don't be afraid to challenge because you can do this constructively. Be proud of who you are and be happy.*
Kirsten	*Trust that you will be where you should be. Be compassionate and curious.*
Sadia	*Embrace your difference and feel empowered to embrace it. Challenge when you need to challenge. It is ok to be different.*
Nilima	*Be who you want to be and be true to yourself. You don't have to be a sheep and follow everyone. Do your own thing. And, believe you are wonderful. You are lovely and special as you are.*
Virginia	*Live in the moment and enjoy your life. Have more fun. Be the best you can be, without having to be competitive. Build that core inner self believe: that is important. Notice what is going on, and be kind.*
Lorella	*Take up space. Find someone to talk to. Find a role model. It's good to be vulnerable, but only be vulnerable with those you can trust. Celebrate who you are.*
Talia	*Accept and value your difference; accept the glamour. Be compassionate and understand how hard it is for your parents.*

In some respects so much has changed. When my children started primary school, their classes were so diverse and mixed, the well-intentioned comment when my husband and I got married, that our children would not know what culture they belonged to seemed wholly irrelevant.

We know there is still a lot to do, however, and my invitation to you, the reader, is to take these rich stories, reflect on them and use them as a foundation to identify action. What small deeds can you commit to?

My advice to my younger self would mirror much of what we heard from the women, and I offer this advice to all young people who are and feel different.

Be grateful for the rich heritage you bring. Be confident. Don't make yourself small, but stand proud. Take your place as children of the global majority, but do this not in anger and with a focus on division, but through an exploration of self and celebration of our shared humanity. Connect deeply with your fellow human beings. Connect with the earth.

In the words of Michelle Obama (2018) "Let's invite one another in. Maybe then we can begin to fear less, to make fewer wrong assumptions, to let go of the biases and stereotypes that unnecessarily divide us."

References

Agarwal, P. (2020) *Unravelling Unconscious Bias*. London: Bloomsbury.

Angelou, M. (1978) Still I Rise. The Poetry Foundation www.poetryfoundation.org/poems/46446/still-i-rise (Accessed 15 September 2023).

BBC Proms (2023) Prom 18: Lata Mangeshkar: Bollywood Legend. 28 July. Royal Albert Hall.

Braitwaite, C. (2012) Even in the Playground, I Was Told My Skin Was Too Dark: It's Time to Face Up to Colourism. *The Guardian* www.theguardian.com/world/2021/feb/27/time-to-face-up-to-colourism-candice-brathwaite (Accessed 15 September 2023).

Brandt, A. (2021) 9 Things You Need to Know About Shame. www.psychologytoday.com/us/blog/mindful-anger/202111/9-things-you-need-to-know-about-shame (Accessed 15 September 2023).

Brown, B. (2010) *The Gifts of Imperfection*. Center City, MN: Hazelden Information & Educational Services.

Chisholm, S. (1969) Speech at Howard University. Washington, DC. 21 April. American Radioworks. https://americanradioworks.publicradio.org/features/blackspeech/schisholm-2.html (Accessed 7 January 2023).

Clance, P. R. and Imes, S. (1978) The Imposter Phenomenon in High Achieving Women: Dynamic's and Therapeutic Intervention. *Psychotherapy Theory, Research and Practice*, 15(3): 1–8.

Clark, K. and Clark, M. (1947) The Clark Doll Test of the 1940s Shows how the Mind Can be Programmed in Negative Ways. YouTube. www.youtube.com/watch?v=y-TYFCsMQp2c&t=1s (Accessed 15 March 2023).

Cox, J. (2023) The Perfect Storm Keeping Women of Colour Behind at Work, Equality Matters. British Broadcasting Corporation. www.bbc.com/worklife/article/20230228-the-perfect-storm-keeping-women-of-colour-behind-at-work (Accessed 7 January 2024).

Duske, S. (2016) Toxic Culture 101: Understanding the Sexualization of Women Ms. Magazine.https://msmagazine.com/2016/01/04/toxic-culture-101-understanding-the-sexualization-of-women/ (Accessed 19 September 2023).

Evaristo, B. (2019) *Girl, Woman, Other*. London: Hamish Hamilton.

Goff, A., Jackson, M. C., Allison, B., Di Leone, L., Curlotta, C. M. and Di Tomasso, N. A. (2014) The Essence of Innocence: Consequences of Dehumanizing Black Children. *Journal of Personality and Social Psychology*, 106(4): 526–545.

Harris, K., Krygsman, S., Waschenko, J. and Rudman, D. L. (2017) Ageism and the Older Worker: A Scoping Review. *The Gerontologist*, 58(2) April 2018: e1–e14. https://doi.org/10.1093/geront/gnw194 (Accessed 19 September 2023).

Kaufman, G. (2004) *The Psychology of Shame: Theory and Treatment of Shame-Based Syndromes*. New York: Springer Publishing Company.

Kiner, M. (2020) It's Time to Break the Cycle of Female Rivalry, *Harvard Business Review*. https://hbr.org/2020/04/its-time-to-break-the-cycle-of-female-rivalry (Accessed 19 September 2023).

Kinouani, G. (2021) *Living While Black: The Essential Guide to Overcoming Racial Trauma*. London: Penguin Random House.

Lewis, M., and Ramsay, D. (2002) Cortisol Response to Embarrassment and Shame. *Child Development*, 73(4): 1034–1045.

Lewis-Oduntan, C. (2020) Black British Mums on The Tough Reality of Raising Sons In the UK. www.refinery29.com/en-gb/black-british-motherhood-son (Accessed 15 September 2023).

Nandi, A., Luthra, R. and Benzeval, M. (2020) When Does Hate Hurt the Most? Generational Differences in the Association Between Ethnic and Racial Harassment, Ethnic Attachment, and Mental Health. *Ethnic and Racial Studies*, 43(16): 327–347, doi: 10.1080/01419870.2020.1788107.

Obama, M. (2018) *Becoming*. New York: Viking.

Phinney, J. S. (1989) Stages of ethnic identity development in minority group adolescents. *Journal of Early Adolescence*, 9(1–2): 34–49.

PwC (2024) Women in Work: Unmasking Inequalities: Delving Deeper into the Gender Pay Gap. Insight. 29 February. https://www.pwc.co.uk/services/economics/insights/women-in-work-index.html (Accessed 5 April 2024).

Raypole, C. (2021) You're Not a Fraud. Here's How to Recognize and Overcome Imposter Syndrome. www.healthline.com/health/mental-health/imposter-syndrome (Accessed 15 September 2023).

Ryan, L. (2023) *Revolting Women: Why Midlife Women Are Walking Out*. Northwich: Practical Inspiration Publishing.

The Runnymede Trust (2020) Race and Racism in Secondary Schools. www.runnymedetrust.org/publications/race-and-racism-in-secondary-schools (Accessed 17 September 2023).

Walker, A. (1983) *In Search of Our Mothers' Gardens*. San Diego: Harvest Books.

Williams, A. (2016) Why We Should Talk to Children About Race. The Conversation. https://theconversation.com/why-we-should-talk-to-children-about-race-59615 (Accessed 23 September 2023).

Woo, D. (2000) *Glass Ceilings and Asian Americans: The New Face of Workplace Barriers*. Walnut Creek, PA: Altamira Press.

YMCA (2020) Young and Black. www.ymca.org.uk/wp-content/uploads/2020/10/ymca-young-and-black.pdf (Accessed 15 September 2023).

3

Hope for a Different Way

There's change when people are told what to do
And change when people choose what to do
Telling imposes control
Asking releases ownership
Changing awareness changes everything
Awareness comes from connecting
Inviting connection, the change arises within
And so it begins.

(Neil Scotton, 2023)

Inextricable Truths (according to my worldview)

In writing this book, I recognise that the act of sharing lived experience and racial trauma is important and I applaud the many before me who have shared personal stories. We know human connection is a key vehicle for change and we recognise that we need to step into the discomfort and stop avoiding the difficult conversations if we are to move forward. We also know that if we expand our definition of 'we' from our immediate group to humanity, and indeed all living beings, we might act very differently.

The world needs us to act differently and find a different way of being on this earth and so in this penultimate part of the book, I explore how we can start to shift from anxiety and despair to a place filled with hope, where instead of the meaningless 24/7 connectivity we have filled our lives with, we can find a deeper way of truly connecting.

In considering this, I want to acknowledge the seminal contribution of Dr Anita Sanchez (2017) in her work *The Four Sacred Gifts*. Based on the wisdom of first nation elders, she names the gifts as:

1. The power to forgive the unforgivable
2. The power of unity

DOI: 10.4324/9781003390602-4

3. The power of healing
4. The power of hope

This feels like a formidable blueprint to guide our thinking. Most powerful for me in the context of the collective impact of Othering is gift 1: the power to forgive the unforgivable. Without this, we are stuck in polarisation, trauma, guilt and shame. Anita describes her journey to first forgive the men and community who killed her father and then ultimately forgive her father for being an imperfect parent, expressing gratitude for her very being. She offers practical solutions including being present, a focus on positive relationships, gratitude and spending time in nature every day, which I certainly try and incorporate into my life, not always successfully.

Anita is not alone in her call to invite us to reconsider and move to a more global lens with which to view the world. A shift from the ego-centric to eco-centric thinking is one way we could change the negative course we are currently charting. The World Economic Forum (2024) commented: "We have developed a dualistic view of our existence on this planet – one that blinds us to our interdependence and inter-connectedness with nature, and which has also created enormous divides in our society and across humanity." Some readers may not immediately see the link between the climate crisis, poverty and racial inequality, but I would argue, our challenges are fundamentally inter-connected and a direct result of our ego-centric approach. This is supported by an organisation to which I belong, The Climate Coaching Alliance (www.climatecoachingalliance.org).

My assertion is that a shift to a collective approach in organisations, where we bring empathy, compassion, accountability and a recognition that we are custodians of the planet, not its owner, will bring about greater racial equality.

This is complex work and there are no easy answers; if there were, we would no doubt have found them by now. Anti-racism initiatives have been numerous and in many nations there is, or has been at moments in time, a real political will to create fairer societies.

Ryde (2019) sums up the probable reason why such initiatives have failed to gain traction, sharing:

■ *We are focussing on trying to give equality of opportunity to black people while not owning up to white privilege.*
■ *We are saying that this a problem for black people who need our help.*
■ *Racist attitudes go underground because people privately have different attitudes to the ones they acknowledge publicly.*
■ *Racist attitudes are often unconscious so that even people concerned about these issues are not necessarily aware of their racism.*

Anyone who has done any work in the area of inclusion will recognise the above. The best programmes, in my view, focus on the fourth element Ryde identifies, bringing our biases from unconscious to conscious as a starting point. The art of active and lifelong reflection really does feel like an essential component if we are to increase our awareness and move to action. Self-work feels like the key to unlock a different way of connecting to others. We also need to feel we do not have to mask or pretend, and in this reflection on authenticity, I can also relate to Ryde's third point. I remember clearly working with a people of colour group and one participant saying: "I will know we have succeeded when people can offer different views about race. At the moment people are still saying what they think they should say."

It is easy to find the ask overwhelming, but everywhere there are kernels of hope and writers and thinkers offering potential ways forward. In some cases, direct and spontaneous action can also remind us of the possibilities.

A prominent example in history which was symbolic in terms of demonstrating the power of the collective was the so-called "Battle of Cable Street". In the 1930s in Stepney, in the East End of London, there was a large Jewish community, many of whom fled the Pogroms in Russia and in Europe more widely. Rosenberg (2021) writing on the eighty fifth anniversary of the event describes Sir Oswald Mosley's rise to power, taking advantage of post-depression poverty to build a strong fascist movement in the UK, known as the British Union of Fascists (BUF). By all accounts, Mosley modelled himself on Mussolini and even created a menacing group, known as the "Blackshirts", copying the Italian "Arditi". Much like Mussolini and, of course, the ultimate architect of European fascism, Adolf Hitler, Mosley peddled hate, with a systematic campaign of dehumanising and derogatory language about the Jewish people.

On Sunday 4 October 1936, Mosley had managed to secure permission for a march through Whitechapel, a largely Jewish community, designed to intimidate and send a strong signal that they were not welcome in his vision of a strong new Britain. What followed was a mass movement resisting the march, where Jewish people came out onto the streets in resistance, despite pleas from anxious community leaders to stay at home. They were joined by Irish workers, union members and members of the Communist Party who cancelled a march they were planning in order to redirect their members to the East End. Despite a 100,000-name petition asking for the march to be banned, there was large-scale support at the time from media and police, and so the government ignored this request. Rosenberg describes how, unable to pass on their original route, the Blackshirts attempted to march down Cable Street, which ran in parallel. He states: "Mosley had battled for the hearts and minds of the Irish community but so had the anti-fascists. On that day Irish dockers, in particular, came to the Jewish end of Cable Street to help build barricades." The chant that rang out was "They shall not pass".

In 1970s Britain, young people from Asian grounds formed the Asian youth movements, as a self-organising reaction to the scapegoating of Commonwealth immigrants and an increasing prevalence of violence. The year 1976 was a significant turning point, in that a young man named Gurdip Singh Chaggar was killed in a racist attack, leading to the creation of Southall Youth Movement. The communities felt they were under direct attack and mobilised to defend themselves. In a parallel to the Cable Street events, the National Front in 1976 took to routinely marching in Manningham in Bradford, an area predominantly inhabited by those of Pakistani and Kashmiri origin. Here too a Youth Movement was created, however they went beyond a defensive approach and more actively campaigned for better rights, housing and education. Communities in other large cities such as Manchester followed, with each geographical movement having differing characteristics. Ramamurthy (2016) shares her thoughts that we have a lot to learn from the change created by these communities. At a time when many feel hopeless about the ability to change our society, they offer hope. Ramamurthy concludes with respect to the youth movements: "They challenged the tactics of divide and rule through their broad-based alliances, while embracing the right of oppressed peoples to organise independently in order to have their voice heard." With modern day tactics of divide and rule well and truly at play, the need to coalesce in alliances which cross boundaries feels crucial.

In the current climate, these events do not feel like we can comfortably prescribe them to history. Rosenberg states the need for vigilance in the present day, stating:

> And, perhaps in doing so, we will draw inspiration and ideas from ordinary people who, in the maelstrom of the 1930s, disregarded the hollow advice of those with more comfortable lives and more blinkered vision, and found collective ways to face these problems with such courage, imagination and determination.

The counter to this example of mass action is beautifully illustrated by the famous 1946 poem by Martin Niemöller, a German theologian and pastor. In his poem he writes of the Nazis coming for the communists, the trade unionists and the Jews, with the final line: "Then they came for me. And there was no one left to speak out for me." A compelling and heart-wrenching narrative of the risk of staying silent in the face of injustice, and a salutary lesson we would do well to heed.

In our fragmented society where we feel forced to take sides in our in-groups, it feels hard to make a stand. We can be in multiple 'in-groups', but in each group there is a pressure to conform and agree with the core messaging. This also plays out in society and politically. Life is complicated and ethically difficult to navigate, but increasingly we are not allowed a nuanced viewpoint. I agree with the psychiatrist and writer Johnston, who in 2021 observed:

> Conflict between ideological factions has become so pronounced that real conversation about a great many topics has become largely impossible. Extreme polarization is setting neighbor against neighbor, creating a distraction that gets in the way of addressing essential questions, and often very directly putting us at risk.

In commenting on the polarisation we see, Johnston asserts that we will come to a point of realisation that there are more than two answers, a right and a wrong, when we ask ourselves the big, systemic questions. Johnston also refers to his work on Cultural Maturity, arguing that in order to do what we need to do as a species, we must find a more evolved way of thinking and being. This resonates with a quote I have used in my leadership development work from Susan Scott. In her 2009

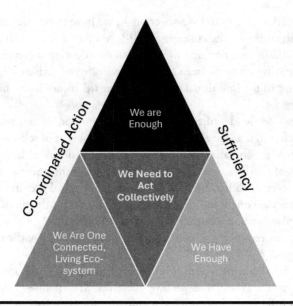

Figure 3.1 Inextricable Truths

book, she states: "The great differentiator going forward, the next frontier for exponential growth, the place where individuals and organizations will find a new and sustainable competitive edge, resides in the area of **human connectivity**." One could extend that to more than humanity, rather all living things.

I also often quote her assertion that all change happens one conversation at a time. Back to generative conversations as a key enabler of change.

A fundamental skill we need to apply is questioning the status quo and the divisive narrative. In drawing the lessons from events in Cable Street, we would be wise to ask ourselves the question of who benefits from this division? It is easy for this to manifest as cynicism, which is not helpful in moving us forward. I would rather bring a mindset of curiosity and compassion, and a healthy dose of scepticism, to facts that are presented as the single version of the truth.

If we go back to looking more systemically, my reflection on the interconnectedness of our challenges leads me to the following, or what I am choosing to call my version of inextricable truths.

If we were to believe that these are indeed truths, what might that enable and what is the work we need to do?

We Are Enough

Earlier, I shared the evidence that the way society is structured, leads to a propensity to be dissatisfied or feel shame. We judge worth by comparison and our tendency to Other leads us to diminish our shared humanity.

It feels intuitive that to feel we are enough, we have to practice self-love. When I looked for literature on the concept of self-love there was very little to be found. Underwood (2020), in a doctoral thesis, set out to develop a consensus definition of self-love, drawing on work from seminal psychologists such as Fromm and Rogers. The concept of unconditional positive self-regard comes from the work of Carl Rogers.

Underwood clearly identifies love for self as an individual and relational or dual process, and refers to it as "an authentic, unconditional type of self-love which makes the task of loving others easier, not more difficult". He distinguishes this from more negative views of self-love, which places self-love with selfishness and narcissism. If we relate this to race, and go back to the construct of social identity theory, we can reasonably draw the conclusion that in order to fully accept the humanity of others, we must first place value on ourselves. This value needs to be genuine and unconditional. It does not require us to own a certain size house or a particular car or have titles and badges.

Reflecting on the evidence from humanistic psychology, it is my belief that we can only love others as much as we love ourselves. We are ill-equipped to be fully empathetic to others if we do not have empathy for ourselves. If this is true, our capacity to build compassionate, authentic relationships with others may be limited by our lack of self-worth. If this is indeed a constraining factor, what, if anything, can we do to increase our capacity for self-love?

Greenberg (2017) identifies the following key elements:

1. **Mindfulness**: Having an open, curious, non-judging attitude; not over-identifying with negative stories about the self.
2. **Self-kindness**: Treating yourself kindly, rather than harshly. Extending the same care and support to yourself that you would to a good friend or loved one.
3. **Common humanity**: Allowing yourself to be human, to make mistakes and learn from them. Knowing that as humans we are not perfect, nor should we be expected to act flawlessly.

She talks about the positive outcomes and shares: "Self-compassion is much more effective in changing behavior than trying to motivate yourself with *shame* and self-criticism."

I think we can all relate to the point about treating ourselves with the kindness we apply to those dear to us, or in my case, this would include clients. In my coaching, I often suggest mindfulness practice and gratitude journals, and I talk about the importance and inter-connection of physical wellbeing with mental wellbeing. I also often do not practice what I preach!

Edmondson (2023), in her book *The Right Kind of Wrong*, invites us to accept the learning offered by failure and our human fallibility, reframing this as a strength and a natural partner to our creativity and drive.

For me, the key things that stand out and we, therefore, need to work on, are being open and non-judgemental, taking care of self and developing a growth mind-set. We need to believe the mantra that we are enough, without the artificial status the trappings of wealth give us. We need to believe, as people of the global majority, that we can rise above systemic injustice and also believe in our worth.

Not everyone can do this, but my genuine belief is most people can. It is not easy, but it is possible. And this could shift the dial. Brown (2017) states hopefully her belief that: "Most of us can build connection across difference and fight for our beliefs if we're willing to listen and lean into vulnerability."

For those so tied up in the net of racial trauma or white fragility, others can, and I hope will, do the work for you.

We Have Enough

Earlier, I mentioned the work of Lynne Twist and her concept of sufficiency. The theory of degrowth economics has been with us for decades. Victor Frankl in his 2019 book *Yes to Life in Spite of Everything* states: "In the economic system of the last few decades, most working people have been turned into mere means, degraded to become mere tools for economic life." This resonates for me. In our unquestioning acceptance of modern economic theory and a focus on growth, we have somehow allowed our human potential to be diminished. I strongly believe there is another way. Mastini (2017) purports: "Degrowth means primarily the abolition of economic growth as a social objective. This implies a new direction for society, one in which societies will use fewer natural resources and will organize and live differently from today." He, like others, questions the perceived association of growth and societal benefit, arguing instead we need to achieve a "right-sizing" between national and local economies, one that takes into account the natural ability of the planet to regenerate. We heard earlier from the work of Schwartz about the so-called paradox of choice. Mastini argues beyond a certain level, it is not more consumerism that makes us happy at a societal level, rather it is income equality. Degrowth is possible by limiting growth, investing in public services and creating a different way of organising society with a focus on cooperation and unpaid labour.

This will not happen without focussed and targeted effort and political will. To create this political will, people of all nations need to look beyond the divisive narrative which is continuously directed at them. They also need to test the logic of the assumptions they are making. Early in 2024, I was listening to the radio and the farmers in France were blockading roads in protest at the perceived lack of support from the government. One individual was interviewed and he said that next time he votes, it will be for the far right. After my initial dismay, I found myself curious about how he was so convinced the far right parties would understand his needs and make his life better. What are the stories he is hearing? What are the truths he is holding to be fact?

One of our key challenges is to craft a compelling story for what degrowth could look like. Rather than a focus on deficit and giving up, the work on active hope could allow us to create a belief in an evolved, more connected and more equitable way of living. Again, storytelling feels like a powerful tool to help us reimagine our way of being.

It will be a journey and we will falter. Our current way of living is hardwired into us. But slowly, we can move to the light.

We Are One Connected, Living Eco-system

We may think of racial inequity, poverty and biodiversity breakdown as unique challenges, but the reality is they are all deeply inter-connected. The UN recognised this in developing the Sustainable Development Goals (SDGs) which take a holistic approach to economic, political, climate and governance opportunities. The supporting Inner Development Goals guide the work we need to do at an individual level.

With neo-liberalism and communism as paradigms come an ego-centric approach, an approach which has led us to place ourselves, that is, humanity, at the head of the table. We need to accept we are part of life on earth, not masters of it. It is so hard for us to see a way of living that is fundamentally different. The fragility of many of our ecosystems is testament to our unspoken strategy for how to live. In 2022, the World Wildlife Fund published a shocking report which shared that since 1970, 69 per cent of the world's species had been lost. We can act, but time is running out. The Executive Summary implores action, stating: "We know that transformational change – game-changing shifts – will be essential to put theory into practice. We need system-wide changes in how we produce and consume, the technology we use, and our economic and financial systems."

This also links to the theory of Gaia, named after the personification of the earth in Greek mythology.

Fideler (2014) talks eloquently of the theory which suggests the Earth is a living entity, sharing that: "Biological evolution is a natural outgrowth of cosmic evolution, and we are able to think only because our own minds and thoughts are woven out of the intelligent patterns of the greater universe." The idea that there is some universal force working to enhance life on earth feels intuitive. Through our acts as humans, we are certainly challenging this regulating system.

Coming back to human behaviour, in the post-pandemic period we saw a phenomenon coined as "the great resignation". Some of this might have been for other reasons, such as ill health, but hundreds of thousands, particularly in the countries of the northern hemisphere, re-evaluated priorities after the life-changing experiences. Of course, the pandemic was terrible in many ways. I, myself, lost my own father prematurely in the first wave of Covid-19. We have already heard that, in terms of inclusion, much progress was lost in the Covid years.

The pandemic did, however, create a shift in perspective for some. We did not need to be at the retail park or mall every weekend. For some, there was a real process of re-connecting with nature. We even realised we would survive if we did not fly off in droves to sunny resorts every summer. And for some, spending more time at home and with family was a positive thing.

In recognising the inter-connectedness of life, one of the key indicators to measure sustainability is the measure of "Earth Overshoot Day". This marks the day each year by which we will have used the resources that the earth can regenerate in that one year. In 2023 the overall date suggested was 1 August. For most so-called developed nations, in 2023, we reach this point around May. Anything June to December is effectively an overdraft on the earth's resources. Interestingly in 2020, the trend was reversed for the first time in half a century. This should offer us some hope. Although in this instance it was forced, it shows us we can change how we live quickly and fundamentally.

In late 2021 and early 2022 the great resignation was at play as many, notably those in the 50–64 age bracket, decided not to re-enter the world of work. These individuals have been somewhat vilified and blamed for problems in the workforce and productivity. It could, however, be part of a more positive shift which is a turn away from economic growth to community asset.

We Need to Act Collectively

What do we then need to do to create a social movement for change?

Thomas-Olalde and Velho (2011) argue: "collective practices, like uniting in antiracist initiatives or migrant organisations as well as artistic, professional and even individual forms of noncompliance, the refusal to accept and reproduce without question the positions which are assigned through Othering, should be multiplied".

This sounds quite radical, but if viewed positively could create the social movement to trigger change. We have already looked at examples of where individuals have come together to take active steps.

The UN Sustainability Goals are admirable in their ambition and the fact there is clear recognition; we need to act together. In this increasingly polarised society, where conflict is common place and communities are turned against each other, it is hard to feel optimistic about this. The SDGs are not uppermost in most people's lives as they go about their daily business. Shards of hope emerge, however. In January 2024, a joint report from McKinsey & Company and the World Economic Forum shared a measure of global cooperation. The Global Cooperation Barometer is made up of five dimensions of global connection: trade and capital, innovation and technology, climate and natural capital, health and wellness, and peace and security. Despite recent blips in health and security, the overall trend is upwards in terms of the levels of global cooperation. As in so much of our lives, the narrative does not necessarily match the facts.

We could see increasing globalisation as a force for change and if mobilised positively, it can lead to sweeping changes. The Black Lives Matters movement went from a group set up in the US by three women to a global experience in 2020. Kernels of positivity do exist if we look and choose to see them.

So often, however, we face the difficult issues, with defensiveness. Guilt and shame are not pleasant companions. We need to accept, however, we are all part of and shaped by the societies we have created. Brown (2017) reminds us: "we are all vulnerable to the slow and insidious practice of dehumanizing, therefore, we are all responsible for recognizing and stopping it".

Let us mobilise, agitate and refocus our energy to stop dehumanising.

It Starts with Self

As a coach, my paradigm is very much informed by the belief that self-reflection is a good thing and is a pre-requisite for growth. On many of the leadership programmes I work on, I stress the importance of starting with a deep awareness of self.

Brown (2017), in her book *Braving the Wilderness*, talks of the dichotomy of true belonging coming when we have the courage to stand alone. She describes her awakening and ultimate acceptance of the fact she did not fit in and was on the outside. She acknowledges she didn't have the systemic disadvantage around race, but there are parallels with the women I interviewed, notably, working through the shame and coming to a place of deep self-compassion.

One framework I have become very interested in is the Inner Development Goals (IDGs). This is a collective effort to identify the skills and attributes needed to deal with the challenges of modern life. The individuals who have come together to form the not-for-profit organisation that co-ordinate work on the inner goals argue that the poly crisis we find ourselves in requires fundamentally different approaches, that are not currently being taught in schools or workplaces. The authors have collectively identified 23 core skills and qualities, under the following five headings:

- Being: Relationship to Self
- Thinking: Cognitive
- Relating: Caring for Others and the World
- Collaborating: Social Skills
- Acting: Enabling Change

The framework is skilfully crafted and I hope the work gains momentum and forms the basis of more core schooling and leadership training.

It does require the ability and willingness to embrace the discomfort. In one skill, "Openness and Learning Mindset" they identify that: "A capacity to be open to learning, re-evaluation and curiosity about alternative ways of perceiving and interpreting various issues requires a sense of identity robust and complex enough not to feel threatened by cognitive dissonance." This is insightful and leaves me instinctively feeling that many people of colour, for all the reasons we have already shared, may not have a robust enough sense of identity to feel safe in doing this work. There needs to be an acknowledgement that some will require more support to get to the point where they are able to step into this space. We need to enable this, otherwise we further exacerbate the inequality we are trying to address.

In order to make progress, we need to be prepared to do the self-work. Kashtan (2014) talks of the work of Marshall Rosenberg, justifying the use of the phrase, "non-violent". She speaks to the fact that this encapsulates the love, but also the courage needed to hold to one's values. It is not easy, and neither is the fundamental principle of non-violence that encourages us to truly accept and honour those with diametrically opposing views. She also shares that the concept of *power over* is so ingrained in our cultural paradigms, it is hard to define *power with*, where all our needs can be met.

I discussed earlier, the social psychology of Othering and our inherent tendency to increase our self-esteem by looking down on people who are not like us. The fact that biologically and socially the odds are stacked against us means dialogue or generative conversations around race require considerable work. This work starts with understanding our own biases and assumptions and accepting the fact we are all perfectly imperfect. Going back to Greenberg's assertion, we need to accept that we will get things wrong. That requires us to make ourselves vulnerable, which can be deeply uncomfortable. I often find myself saying to participants, "lean into the discomfort" without really thinking about it. But, as I reflect, leaning into discomfort is, in my view, a fundamental requirement in this work.

Entering this place of discomfort is potentially freeing. Macy and Brown (2014) talk of cultural awakening and say we should aim to "raise the consciousness of whites and help them from the soul constricting prisons of ethnic and racial privilege". I am sure some would be cynical about the advantages of shedding privilege.

Kahneman (2012) in his book, *Thinking, Fast and Slow*, introduces us to the concept of System 1 and System 2 thinking. System 1 thinking is automatic, relatively effortless and based on the shortcuts or heuristics we discussed earlier. System 2 thinking is cognitive and requires more effort. Deep self-reflection requires System 2 thinking, that is, it requires effort and energy. Our brains are wired to minimise effort and, therefore, we have a natural resistance to doing the work and making ourselves uncomfortable. This is partly caused by a primeval emotion: fear. Menakem (2017) names this primeval thinking structure as "The Lizard Brain" and he makes the link to racialised trauma, calling white body supremacy "a toxic chemical we ingest on a daily basis".

In order to open ourselves up to conversations about race, we need to overcome our fear and our socialised idea that all conversation should be harmonious. We should seek out and truly hear the stories of people who are different from us. Holding the compassion and positive regard is not always an easy task. I find it helps to reframe my judgement into curiosity. It still takes effort to try and understand, not judge.

For me, this takes me back to Sanchez's power to forgive the unforgiveable as a key aspiration. Forgiveness is vital in moving us forward. Martin Luther King Jr (1963) summed this up beautifully in his statement:

> We must develop and maintain the capacity to forgive. He who is devoid
> of the power to forgive is devoid of the power of love. There is some

good in the worst of us and some evil in the best of us. When we discover this, we are less prone to hate our enemies.

In terms of our social psychology, we are programmed to want to work collectively. We feel a deep need to belong and if we can expand our sense of belonging from affinity groups to the whole human race, we can change our outlook.

Moving to Active Hope

We need to find hope for the future. Frankl (2019) talks of our growing fatalism as humanity, sharing that we have become more sceptical and pessimistic as we can no longer assume a better future. He calls us to challenge the negative, fatalistic mindset with "another propaganda that must be firstly individual and secondly active. Only then can it be positive." This is amplified by Macy and Brown (2014) who implore us to active hope and state: "we can still act for the sake of a liveable world". They offer a more optimistic view of the human condition, urging activism to allow us to "come home to each other and our mutual belonging in the living body of Earth".

I talked earlier of the importance of belonging and the risk that by developing "in-groups" we Other those outside our circle. What if we could elevate our thinking about belonging as a deep connection to all others and to the Earth?

Bolte Taylor (2021) identifies parts of our brain as characters in her compelling book of life and regeneration, following a stroke. She talks of shifting to right brain thinking, or higher consciousness as an uncomfortable but necessary part of our growth. She shares: "Embarking on this part of the journey is often the most difficult step, as it requires us to recognise and admit that our small-self-ego-brain must step to the side if we are to grow beyond what we currently are."

Macy and Brown (2014) offer us a plethora of practices, in chapters headed "Coming from Gratitude", "Honouring Our Pain for the World", "Seeing with New Eyes" and "Going Forth". These are visceral and active exercises, which use art, imagery and words, often intended to be practiced in community with a guide. As with so much in our lives, we have the tools and the technology; the question is do we have the will and capacity to change our collective thinking?

Joanna Macy earlier identified with Chris Johnstone the phrase "The Great Turning" to describe the seismic shift or ecological revolution which is already underway.

They identified three necessary, not necessarily sequential things that are required of us.

The first was "holding actions", actions to reduce the destruction and maintain what we can of our ecosystems. The second is "life sustaining systems and practices", which involves transforming our structures, actions and the choices we make. The change we need to see in the world will only, however, be realised with the third dimension, a "shift in consciousness". Such a shift requires us to reconnect to our humanity and engage in the personal and spiritual development which allows us to embed a new way of being.

This resonates with indigenous wisdom, and the sharing of women such as Dr Anita Sanchez. Grandmother Medicine Song (2023) speaks of Hopi culture and shares the view we are between the 4th and the 5th worlds, at a point of potential and hope. She believes: "To manifest forward the new 5th World, we need to dream the same dream. If we dream it together, we can bring forward something truly remarkable." We do this by mending the Sacred Hoop and rebalancing with Mother Earth. Aboriginal culture also talks of the dreaming process and the survival of the human spirit. Deep in the hearts of our communities, there is ancient knowing which in our consumerist, ego-based world, we have somehow lost.

A Relational Space

Humans connecting as humans sounds so simple. Why, then, are we so bad at it? Generative dialogue requires us to notice and question our assumptions and in the words of Nancy Kline, "listen with fascination". We bridge the gaps by sharing our experiences. Kubin et al. (2021) concluded in a study about how best to connect across difference: "furnishing perceptions of truth within moral disagreements is better accomplished by sharing subjective experiences, not by providing facts".

We all have a responsibility to seek out diverse human stories. I fundamentally believe this is one of our key tools in reducing Othering. A deep belief in the power of individual stories is one of the things which drove me to write this book. Telling our stories is important to create societal change; it is also healing. I am a huge fan of Marshall Ganz and his model of Public Narrative. He argues societal change can be achieved through consideration of The Story of Self; The Story of Us and the Story of Now. This comprises a consideration of what calls you as an individual, a sense of collective and a call to action in terms of urgency to act, in the moment. Storytelling is built into our DNA and remains an important tool for connection and knowledge exchange. Amanda Gorman, the youngest inaugural American poet concludes that storytelling is not just about entertainment, it is primarily about empathy. She shared in 2022:

> Finding empathy is a difficult challenge but also the most human of the reasons we tell stories. Often, we explain and express so that we can be seen or so that others can empathize with us. Often, effective persuading means truly stepping into another's point of view.

Storytelling is a powerful way for us to connect as humans and heal, sharing stories from our past to help shape our futures.

For immigrants, storytelling is all the more important as it is a way of connecting to communities of birth and identity. It can form a necessary anchor in unfamiliar environments and build the mesh of new communities.

Brown (2017) has a wonderfully titled chapter: "People are Hard to Hate Close Up: Move In". She addresses the dehumanising behaviours which precede racial inequality, talking about language, imagery and societal norms. If we move from thinking about the Other to thinking about people we actually know, we have a much more nuanced view of individual value. Getting to know people as people, rather than someone from a different group, is a fundamental part of shifting the dial. Gaither and Sommers (2013) conducted research with American college students, tracking the attitudes of white students who shared a room with an other-race, rather than a same-race fellow student. They found that those who had lived in close proximity to an other-race individual were subsequently more inclusive in their behaviour, stated they valued diversity more and were less anxious in novel interracial situations. This was measured robustly and went beyond previous attitudinal based research. They concluded: "Residential contact with other-race individuals not only affects race-related attitudes, but can also reduce interracial anxiety and positively influence behaviour in subsequent diverse settings." The researchers suggest that this could form part of the strategy to create communities where diversity is valued. My own experience of living in University Halls of Residence would support this. For some, this was the first time they had lived side by side with people from very different communities and backgrounds. Maybe I was lucky with the accommodation block I was in, but we lived fairly harmoniously, and a few of my neighbours are still good friends. If people live in segregated areas and do not have the opportunities to move close, it is much easier to stay in a place of fear, suspicion and anxiety.

Tropp and Godsil (2014) also found that "Extensive psychological research shows that we can reduce racial anxiety when we reach beyond our segregated friendship circles or communities and cultivate meaningful relationships with people of other races." They state that the more contact is repeated, the greater the positive impact in terms of a reduction in anxiety. Of course, this is not to say that we do not have to address systemic issues, but creating an environment where individuals from different cultures live, work and play together can lead to a situation where "We can all benefit from moving beyond the confines of our group boundaries into a broader circle of relationships, friendships, and colleagues."

In some respects, we are more global in our outlook, but the reality is we still often primarily interact with people who are like us. We are drawn to the comfort of the familiar.

Building connection through good conversation requires us to be in close proximity with people who are different. The last few decades have seen a move away from integrated approaches to education, with more faith schools opening in many European countries. If children don't spend time with people from different backgrounds and faiths, they are much more likely to see them as Other. This initiative has potentially taken us back considerably. The focus on individual choice, rather than what creates a fair society, will create a generation of children where a sizeable minority will have little or no contact with children outside of their immediate community. This cannot be a good thing in my view. Some are trying to redress this, with organisations such as the Council for Integrated Education campaigning and working to support the growth of integrated schools in Northern Ireland. As well as four core principles, they commit to five important factors:

- People-led
- Intentional about Inclusion
- Student Centred
- Aspirational
- Committed to Fairness

I am drawn to their language and focus on a "shared society".

In developing their approach to social responsibility, they have declared the following commitment:

> The integrated school delivers the curriculum on an all-ability and inclusive basis to all of its pupils. It respects the uniqueness of every pupil and acknowledges his/her entitlement to personal, social, intellectual and spiritual development in the attainment of individual potential. This philosophy affirms that pupils should be encouraged to:
>
> (a) understand and engage with the use of non-violent means of conflict resolution;
> (b) demonstrate mutual respect and understanding towards others, and develop tolerance and trust of those who are different;
> (c) nurture self-confidence and self-respect;
> (d) appreciate the interdependence between society and the natural environment it inhabits.

This example of how education has been transformed in Northern Ireland in a relatively short period offers hope for the future. The approach feels so aligned to my views, I wish that their reach could be expanded far and wide.

Even in the darkest moments of history, there is coalition and hopefulness. In the midst of the conflict in Gaza in early 2024, I became aware of a movement in Israel called Standing Together, bringing Jews and Palestinians together to call for peace. Their inspiring approach was based on their collective belief: "While the minority who benefit from the status quo of occupation and economic inequality seek to keep us divided, we know that we – the majority – have far more in common than that which sets us apart." The organisation has brought together Israelis and Palestinians in commune to share their grief in safety and togetherness. One of their stated missions is: "re-humanizing the discourse, retaining humanity, mourning all lives lost". Retaining our humanity, or arguably rediscovering it, feels like a good focus for our collective work.

Having conversations across difference is clearly a good thing if we want to reduce exclusion. How we have the conversations is important. Balboa and Glaser (2018) share the thoughts of Judith Glaser, suggesting there are three different types of conversations. Transactional conversations are primarily about information exchange. Level 2 is positional conversations which start to bring in some enquiry, but the starting point is to defend or reinforce our position, or our version of the truth. The third level is more akin to the earlier definition of generative conversations. Level 3 is transformation, where new insights emerge. This is where we need to strive to get to in conversations with people of different cultures and races. To enable this we need to quickly develop trust. The researchers share work on neuroscience and suggest that as people communicate, our neural systems connect, and if they are aligned this helps us to build trust and understanding. Asking discovery questions, deep listening and consistency of words and body language all shift our response from a stress response to a positive feelgood response.

Earlier I looked at the ability for generative conversations to create new meaning and insights. To do this, we must bring curiosity, attention and deep listening to our exchanges.

It appears talking is not simple and we need to practice the art of conversation and intentionally create opportunities for shared learning. Organisations like The Human Library may well offer us a roadmap for this dialogue. They are a global not-for-profit organisation aimed at creating safe spaces for people to challenge differing views around inclusion. I, myself, took part in an event and it was incredibly impactful; definitely the only form of speed dating I would ever consider. I was impressed with the courage of the participants and found myself very at ease in telling my story. This was in 2017 and for me was, in part, the catalyst which allowed me to be more comfortable in talking about the impact of race from a personal perspective.

From Me to We

Harrell (2018) describes the opportunities if we can rise above our ego-centric approach and embrace diversity in its broadest sense. She concludes: "The strength of diversity and multi-culturalism lies in the ability to simultaneously honor and transcend differences in order to promote social justice and contribute to progressing humanity forward."

Only through believing in a different future can we shift to realise it.

A helpful framework is Milton Bennett's 1986 model, revised several times over the years, where he introduces the Developmental Model of Intercultural Sensitivity (DMIS). This offers a continuum based on grounded theory, through observation of how individuals respond in intercultural training situations, with a focus on how worldview is internalised. This is consistent with the concept of social constructivism, highlighted earlier in this book. The model can be applied as an individual diagnostic or to assess the culture of organisations.

Bennett identifies different stages of intercultural maturity, which are:

Denial: This is clearly linked to Othering, where sameness is valued and other cultures are not accepted or respected as equal.

Defence: Here difference is accepted but in a way that is stereotypical and often approached with hostility. This too is a place associated with Othering.

Minimisation: Here the differences are perceived, but reduced, with a shift in focus to similarity. This is the place of "I don't see colour". This masks or hides racial inequality and, therefore, means effective action is not taken.

Acceptance: This begins to move to a position of equality, where individuals recognise their own culture is different to others, but they believe other cultures are equally rich, while being different.

Adaptation: This position is primarily associated with a place of empathy; of recognising others' worldviews and being able to place yourself in their shoes. At an organisational level, adaptation is linked to inclusive behaviours, policies and approaches.

Integration: This is the most evolved stage in the continuum and is associated with the internalisation of complex and changing intercultural perspectives, where individual reality exists in a state between boundaries.

Bennett concludes:

> Cultural liminality can be used to construct cultural bridges and to conduct sophisticated cross-cultural mediation. Organizations at Integration encourage the construction of third-culture positions based on mutual adaptation in multicultural work groups, with the anticipation that thirdculture solutions generate added value.

Thirdculture in this context relates to people who live in a different culture from that of their parents and have often lived in many global cultures. They are otherwise known as diasporic, which originally means scattered. Integration here is absolutely not akin to assimilation where we shift to sameness; it is about creating something new from our wonderful diversity.

Bennett's model can be used as a diagnostic tool, but the challenge in terms of action is to consider how we help individuals and organisations shift to a place of integration. Several Diversity, Equity and Inclusion scales do exist, but there are very few organisations globally which have moved from the transactional to a more transformed and embedded approach. My strong belief remains that human connection and storytelling is the key to tipping the balance. Silvestri (2023) writing in *Psychology Today* shares his view that:

> Stories provide poetic forms to explore the influences of legacy; the mystical influential and aesthetic energy from our families of origin as well as the collective reservoir of our human evolution. They bring to life the contextual interchanges that eventually give relational meaning to ethnicity, race, class, culture, identity and wealth.

By sharing our stories, each individual in the interaction is somehow changed and we move from individual to collective consciousness.

Somatic Approaches

In this book, I have offered the view that the way to reduce Othering and the systemic impact of inequality is through a dialogic process. While at a societal level, I still believe this to be true, for those who are in a place of trauma response this may not be enough. We need to move from head to heart. There is growing interest in the field of therapy using embodied approaches. Dr Peter Levine (2010), a key proponent of somatic approaches, suggests that all too often we focus on rational or cognitive approaches to healing trauma, when trauma by its nature is something that happens to the whole body, not just the mind. His assertion is that in order to unravel trauma in a compassionate and safe way, one must start with the body. Levine argues that the body has a natural ability to heal, but it also has a natural ability to adopt a strategy of paralysis when faced with traumatic events. In biological terms, this is meant to be a temporary strategy, but what sometimes happens is this can become a permanent or stuck state. He discusses the tendency to freeze in situations which would not elicit that reaction in others. In his beautifully crafted and personal book, *In an Unspoken Voice; How the Body Releases Trauma and Restores Goodness*, Levine states: "paralysis becomes a default response to a wide variety of situation in which one's feelings are highly aroused". He also talks of the need for "titration", that is introducing the experience of the trauma slowly and by parts, in order to reduce any negative effects of memory of trauma. This has profound implications for how we think about healing from racial trauma and how we design interventions.

Levine talks of the unhelpful medicalisation of trauma as a disease of the mind, arguing that to move forward: "requires each of us to connect to our biological commonality as instinctual beings; thus, we are linked not only by common vulnerability to fright but our innate capacity to transform such experiences". This resonates with my earlier assertion that we are ruled, in some respects, by our biology. Levine's therapeutic intervention, coming out of his research, is known as "somatic experiencing". An approach that reconnects us with our bodies and encourages us to notice our physical responses to feelings may well be an important part of the armoury in designing effective interventions.

In 2023, I saw Amanda Blake present at an international conference. Her philosophy purports that effectively the body is the brain. She offers us processes to support us in embodied transformation. A gentler approach based on embodiment feels like an exploration we may all benefit from. Soma Essentials, a California-based organisation committed to raising awareness of somatic approaches believe the following:

> somatic psychology can be a powerful tool for self-discovery. By becoming more self-aware and in tune with our bodies, we can gain a deeper understanding of ourselves and our emotions. This can lead to increased self-compassion and a greater sense of well-being. Somatic psychology can also help us identify and release patterns of behavior or thought that may be holding us back from living our best lives.

They also claim practice that incorporates embodiment can improve self-esteem and help us self-manage. If we can internally generate positive self-esteem, is it possible we will feel less need to do this through Othering?

This approach may also be less challenging to individuals who are hesitant to own racial trauma and a good place to start the work we need to do as individuals.

The inter-connection of physical and emotional wellbeing is well accepted, but only recently are we acknowledging the fact the enteric neural system which resides in our intestinal system may serve a greater purpose than digesting our food. The language we have become accustomed to such as trust your gut or butterflies in your stomach may be pointing us to a more fundamental biofeedback process. It is now well accepted that as well as the brain sending messages throughout the body, the gut can send messages to the brain.

Menakem (2017) too advocates a body-based approach to awareness and healing, and indeed he names body practices such as singing, humming, touching and drumming as activities to do individually or in union. He also advocates a mind practice of inviting an ancestor to be with you in your current space. I have tried this practice and found it incredibly powerful. Some other practices he suggests feel less intuitive for those of us brought up in the northern hemisphere, but may be more attuned in other cultures. He suggests a practice of foot washing, stating that through this ritual, we are no longer "Others". I know this would make me feel deeply uncomfortable, as I have a strongly constructed belief that my feet are horrible!

Being in the Moment

Many proponents suggest that our natural fear responses of fight, flight, freeze or fawn can be diminished. Being more mindful and present in the moment can reduce anxiety, improve concentration and prevent unhelpful thought processes, such as overthinking. Cuncic (2024) shares ideas of how to live in the moment, suggesting: "Learning how to be more mindful and live in the moment can give you a greater appreciation for your life, also reducing feelings of stress, depression, and anxiety." She talks of noticing, focussing on one thing at a time, reducing screen time and engaging with nature. We know in our culture of multi-tasking and constant scrolling on phones, we have unlearnt the skill of being in the moment and focussing on one thing at a time. How often do we truly sit and savour every mouthful of a meal, or notice the sounds and sights before us? I encourage readers to experiment and find what brings you to a place of mindfulness. I walk around my pond and watch out for glimpses of the grass carp swimming beneath the surface. Sometimes when I am in my office, I watch the wagtails who seem to have taken to dancing on my car. These activities both noticeably calm my heart rate and slow my need for pace. I am definitely in the space where I do not pay enough attention to being in the moment. I often recommend mindfulness apps to clients, but fail to develop a practice myself. Definitely a work in progress in my life, but I am trying to be less hurried and task-focussed and take time to simply be.

Feminine Energy

This book started as an exploration of women's experiences of being Othered, and I am now drawn back to the fact that the linear thinking which has got us to this point in history is driven by a largely masculine energy. Bashford (2018) in her poetic exploration "You Are a Goddess", relates masculine energy to competition and control, stating: "the dominance of the masculine energy has resulted in global disharmony and lack of equilibrium". By energies, we do not necessarily refer solely to the biological sexes and most would argue, we need a balance of both masculine and feminine energies. I would agree, as humanity, we have chosen to live in imbalance.

If we need a different, more connected way of being, the characteristics associated with female energy; an open heart, forgiveness and a recognition we are part of the whole is what is needed. I come back to Kali Maa, the dark mother, who is so called because before her creations, there was only darkness. She is associated with nature and is seen as all powerful, creating, destroying, but ultimately a benevolent entity. It is not coincidence that Gaia too is often represented as a female force, a goddess.

So, for women now who are activists, what does it mean to awaken the goddess? It arguably starts with acceptance that the cognitive will only take us so far and we need to notice what comes up for us in our hearts; feeling rather than thinking. In our logical, problem-solving world, this intuitive approach has been diminished and devalued. The world right now could do with the female energy which promotes relationship building, forgiving and overcoming conflict.

Self-love, reflective living, creativity and connecting with nature are all ways of celebrating our female energy. Sufficiently resourced, women can come together to challenge the status quo. In my work with other amazing women in the coaching profession, there is an increasing movement of women and men stepping up to challenge the current paradigm, encouraging less ego-centric and more systemic ways of viewing the world.

Wheatley (2024) talks of the concept of *pattern language*, a term born out of architecture but now related to the human spirit. She talks of the patterns as linked to the natural order of life, stating: "The patterns are intrinsic, discerned but not created by human intelligence." She too speaks to a model where we are part of nature, not the controller. She also pivots our understandings of common terms; diversity, inclusion and equality, presenting them as design principles.

> Diversity: Complex issues demand differences to find solutions
> Inclusion: People need to feel needed
> Equality: Begin and end as equals

She welcomes us in her book, *Restoring Sanity*, to a series of practices, inviting us to be "warriors for the human spirit". We don't have to be perfect, rather take time to reflect, experiment and pause to notice and choose the positive path. Wheatley's version of feminine energy is not quiet and acquiescent. It is bold and provocative. She shares a collective view, stating: "In this ruthless environment, what's needed is not individual acts of heroism, but island communities where sanity prevails."

Change will not happen overnight, but if we can start to shift the energy, what might be possible? The wonderful Maya Angelou stated in 2018: "Each time a woman stands for herself, without knowing it, possibly without claiming it, she stands up for all women." We talked earlier about how women often collude in the belief that there is only so much room for women's voices to be heard and our place at the table is at risk if we invite other women in. If we believe a move to feminine energy, the peace bringing approach of connection and forgiveness, is a fundamental way we can heal the world, we must amplify the voice of women. We must use our strong muscles, not to look relevant and toned in the masculine workplaces as Ryan described earlier, but to pull other women into a collective space. A space where we can attempt to generate the dialogue that is needed in our communities and families feels much needed.

Pearce (2016), in her book *Burning Woman*, which is a call to action, states: "These are burning times and they call for Burning Women. This is your time, come out of the shadows and burn brightly."

In their own way, each of the women I interviewed is channelling feminine energy in a way that creates a force for good. The world, possibly, needs more women to become activists.

The Challenges

In my work and exploration in this area, an often overriding emotion is fear. People of colour are fearful because they do not always feel psychologically safe and a sense of belonging, and white people are terrified of being accused of being racist or getting it wrong. This has in many ways led to a paralysis within organisations, which is not serving us well. We have so many diversity initiatives in organisations, but we know inclusion doesn't happen through a compliance approach. We cannot make being inclusive mandatory. It comes from deep work on self, informed by contextual and systemic understanding, and a willingness to move into action. Much of what is on offer around inclusion is just too superficial to make sustainable change. Added to this, there are a number of challenges which strike me.

Is Self-work Starting from the Same Place?

Self-awareness is seen as key to growth, contentment and wellbeing. It is commonplace in caring professions, where we talk of reflective practice, and is seen as a critical part of most leadership programmes. Lucas (2023) makes a statement which resonates so much with me, saying: "Reflection fuels a humility that encourages me to acknowledge multiple perspectives and the inevitability of things unseen. For me, the process enables me to see more than I saw at the time." This feels so critical to the growth mindset and spirit of continuous learning that I hold dear.

But in my more recent work, the doubt has crept in.

Does a focus on self-reflection and the assertion that it is inevitably a good thing also create a systemic barrier for some? Undergoing a process of self-reflection, particularly in a group or team, requires a certain amount of vulnerability. What happens if people do not feel able to do this and might there be unintended consequences?

Ironically one of the best critiques of self-reflection I have encountered is actually framed in the context of personal information tracking and a computing-based approach. Eikey et al. (2021) explored the benefits and risks of self-reflection and collation of data about self and found that in some cases "The reflection process is stifled because users are unable or unwilling to critically analyse their negative emotions and thoughts in order to gain a new perspective." They discuss the fact that self-reflection may lead in some to rumination, where for individuals "They sometimes get trapped in a negative cycle." In other words, instead of reflection being a tool to support a move forward, people get stuck with harmful thoughts.

In the Eikey et al. paper they did not explicitly address race as a factor which might exacerbate the likelihood of rumination rather than developmental self-reflection; however, I am left deeply curious about whether people of colour are more likely to end up in this unhelpful pattern. They do cite evidence that rumination may be linked to adverse life events. Could those events be linked, for some, to racial trauma?

They state: "Characteristics of rumination include being motivated by fear, loss, threats, or self-injustice of the self rather than curiosity or interest in the self." In my work, I have seen people of colour respond defensively in this way. Self-compassion is part of the solution, as too, is the need to feel truly heard. Eikey and colleagues present an interesting suggestion that technology-based solutions may be what helps us in this deeply human and affective space. I, for one, would love to have more answers in terms of supporting individuals who are trapped in this way. I feel a profound sense of sadness and helplessness when I encounter it, and inadequacy in not having the tools to support.

Brown (2017) shares her view that not everyone will become sufficiently resourced to do this work. She states: "Some people will continue to believe that fighting for what they need means denying the humanity of others." Her more positive view is: "Mercifully it will take only a critical mass of people who believe in finding love and connection across difference to change everything."

Stuck in a Trauma Response

Many writers I have already mentioned, such as Menakem and Kinouani, have described the trauma response associated with our social construct of race and racial inequity in detail.

We have also heard of the need for healing to be an active process. For so many, the response is avoidance, which exacerbates the trauma experience, resulting in depression, post-traumatic stress conditions or numbing behaviours, such as substance misuse.

Sadly, some individuals who find themselves in this situation can unconsciously spread the pain, like a random spray of bullets, impacting negatively on those around them.

It is commonly believed that therapy and somatic approaches can support individuals to emotionally process the pain of traumatic events, however, not everyone has access to these supportive tools. Another manifestation of systemic injustice is those living in poverty are more likely to need support and less likely to have the resources to access it.

For any readers who may be stuck in racial trauma, my hope for you is that you find the internal and external resourcing to do the work. It may be a painful process, but the pain of staying stuck will be greater.

The Race Card

Khilay (2012) writes about something which is rarely addressed in any dialogue around race in the workplace, probably because we are too scared to even name it. She names it as "playing the race card". She states one definition of this: "Deliberately and falsely accusing another person of being racist in order to gain some form of advantage." She also talks of the risk of managers overcompensated and being too lenient due to fear of being called racist. This leads to a complex interplay, where some people of colour may well be advantaged. This could, in turn, lead to unhelpful behaviours, and a small minority may well adopt this strategy. I have seen this, in the past, and it has left me deeply affected, a visceral reaction so complex, I find it hard to articulate. A mixture of anger, guilt and shame.

For people of colour who have experienced systemic injustice in their lives, is it really so surprising that they will take advantage where it is offered? Can an advantage generated through some else's fear ever lead to truly positive, enriching relationships? How do we reconcile realities that might be so different, and can we ever really fully conclude whether racism did or did not occur? These are big questions I am grappling with, and as yet, I have no definitive answers.

What Khilay also surfaces, however, is that generalising from cases where race has been brought up inappropriately can negate the real experiences of racism, and this is something we need to guard against. It would be easy to imagine that those who are activists in racial justice in organisations become Othered and labelled as trouble-makers. This, too, I have witnessed. Most people I have encountered who work in inclusion, however, are deeply frustrated by the small number of people who use race as a smokescreen or somehow weaponise it. It makes all our work more difficult.

I wonder what Sanchez's Power of Healing means in this space? I have tried using Marshall Rosenberg's (2015 [1999]) model of non-violent communication.

This seems deceptively simple, but is focussed on the expression and acknowledgement of needs, with a starting premise that most people are good.

He identifies five stages of the practice:

1. Expressing our own needs.
2. Sensing the needs of others, regardless of how they are expressing themselves.
3. Checking to see whether needs are accurately being received.
4. Providing the empathy people need in order to hear the needs of others.
5. Translating proposed solutions or strategies into positive action language.

He uses "need" as a phrase to describe the basic things we need to resource us and argues that all humans effectively have the same needs; we just have different strategies to fulfil them. My experience facilitating based on this approach is that it requires people to at least be in some space of togetherness and it takes time. It can, however, be an extremely impactful way of shifting from polarisation and blame.

The Role of Coaching

I am a coach; I love being a coach; I feel privileged to be a coach and I feel a responsibility to use my practice for good. I find myself curious about the role of coaching in co-creating the solution.

Hawkins and Turner (2020) state:

> For coaching to help create the next revolution in leadership development, it needs to help leaders develop 'WeQ' – collective and collaborative intelligence – and to integrate individual, group and team coaching into leadership development programmes that are based on delivering value, not just to participants but also to the current and future stakeholders of their leadership.

A systemic approach to coaching practice, by its very nature, encourages leaders to think beyond their own needs and to notice inter-connection. This is critically important if we are to shift from our current growth paradigm.

Wheatley (2024) talks of "sane leadership", recognising the challenge of leadership in the current climate, but arguing that difficult though the work of reawakening the human spirit is, it is the only work worth doing.

Coaches can and, I believe, should use their skills to create awareness and work with leaders systemically to allow them to focus on creating social value, not wealth for the few. There is not a debate about our agenda and the client's agenda: the agenda is humanity.

If coaching is to be a tool to support the evolution of humanity, it feels like it needs to be more diverse in its offering.

Shah (2022), in a groundbreaking book about inclusion in coaching, shares her insights of working with and being intensely curious about an individual's lived experience. Sensitivity and empathy are required to understand the systems individuals operate in, together with a deep acceptance that others' priorities may be very different to our own. Shah argues that all coaches need to have the ability to work in a way which actively supports inclusion. She also prioritises the delivery of coaching training offers which specifically target people from minoritised communities.

It saddens me to see so many coaching courses which still have cursory or no content on inclusion and belonging. Coaching professional bodies are talking about the issue, but progress feels very slow and I often meet coaches who have little understanding of intersectionality and concepts of power and privilege.

In terms of how we use coaching for social good and reducing Othering, I invite coaches to be more intentional in where we put our individual attention. I offer no judgement, but I have no interest in coaching an individual who wants to make Partner in a professional services firm. I would much rather divert my energy and resources to leaders who want to create inclusive environments, lead for social change or to drive Wheatley's concept of sane leadership.

We can work with leaders to realise the goal of making our large institutions more inclusive. As coaches we need to be courageous. We will get things wrong and we may use language that does not resonate, but if we go into the space with curiosity and compassion we can change organisational culture and better support people of colour or the global majority to succeed and thrive in their lives and work. As organisations are in many cases reducing investment in specific DE&I initiatives, it is all the more important that those of us responsible for working in the space of leadership development embed inclusion into our core work. It really is everyone's business and it is important that we as coaches take this seriously in our continued professional development.

I also believe that those coaches who take somatic approaches are instrumental in healing and racial justice. Supporting people on a journey to a place where their nervous system is not in hyper-alert or freeze mode feels like a good focus for our talents. I appreciate all those coaches who work in this space.

Finally, as well as the self-work, we need to think about resourcing ourselves. For me, working in inclusion, supervision has been essential in grounding me, allowing a safe space for me to express pain and frustration and supporting my reflective practice. Supervisors, too, need to be trained to work skilfully in this space. I am fortunate; I have an amazing supervisor and I always leave our sessions feeling lighter.

What Is the Social Movement We Now Need?

We have heard of the success of social movements, and there are numerous examples to this day of where groups have come together to champion a cause. In the inclusion space, the most well-known movement is probably Black Lives Matters;

however, despite my huge admiration for them, can we really conclude there has been a hugely positive impact?

The problem may be that we tackle issues individually rather than recognising they are inter-connected in nature and we are facing a polycrisis. The term polycrisis relates to the layering effect of multiple negative events and challenges arising at once.

The solution may well be about greater connection, joining up efforts, with both individuals, but crucially organisations and governments coming together in unprecedented ways. UNICEF in 2023 suggest the focus should be on children, stating that: "Ultimately, a coordinated and collective effort is needed to protect the rights and well-being of children. This includes not only providing immediate assistance but also addressing the underlying causes of the polycrisis and building resilience for the future."

We need to pivot power away from the 2024 Forbes estimate of 2781 billionaires in the world and pay attention to future generations. All of them. In every nation, in every community. We need to truly hear them and involve them in decision making. I mentioned earlier the vitriol directed at Greta Thunberg. The individuals at the beginning of any movement are often ridiculed or vilified, but maybe those of us with any sort of power need to support young people to face the challenges that we are collectively ignoring. We are doing young people a disservice in not preparing them for a very different future.

My belief is that we need to fundamentally rethink our approach to governance and empower communities to take control and be less passive. The Global Assembly Movement aims to fundamentally campaign for this shift. In doing so, it very much reconnects with indigenous processes of community decision making and consensus approaches. This creates a system on governance which remains mindful of the world consequences of each decision; decisions made with love, not with certainty. To create an inclusive society, we need a society which truly democratises and distributes power. I invite you, the reader to consider: what is your part to play in this movement?

References

Angelou, M. (2018) cited by International Peace Bureau Youth Network. https://ipbyn.org/2018/11/21/each-time-a-woman-stands-for-herself-without-knowing-it-possibly-without-claiming-it-she-stands-up-for-all-women/ (Accessed 15 March 2024).

Balboa, N. and Glaser, R. D. (2018) The Neuroscience of Conversations. www.psychologytoday.com/gb/blog/conversational-intelligence/201905/the-neuroscience-of-conversations (Accessed 15 May 2023).

Bashford, S. (2018) *You Are a Goddess: Working with the Sacred Feminine to Awaken, Heal and Transform*. California: Hay House Inc.

Bennett, M. (2017) Developmental Model of Intercultural Sensitivity. The IDR Institute. www.idrinstitute.org/wp-content/uploads/2019/02/DMIS-IDRI.pdf (Accessed 12 February 2024).

Blake, A. (2023) Embodied Self Awareness. Presented at Coaches Rising Conference, October 2023. www.coachesrising.com/podcast/embodied-self-awareness-with-amanda-blake/

Bolte Taylor, J. (2021) *Whole Brain Living, The Anatomy of Choice and the Four Characteristics that Drive Our Life*. London: Hay House UK.

Brown, B. (2010) *The Gifts of Imperfection*. Minnesota: Hazelden Information & Educational Services.

Brown, B. (2017) *Braving the Wilderness*. London: Penguin Random House

Council For Integrated Education (n.d.) The Integrated Ethos. Northern Ireland. https://nicie.org/what-is-integrated-education/integrated-ethos/ (Accessed 10 December 2023).

Cuncic, A. (2024) How to Live in the Moment: Ways to Be More Present in Your Everyday Life. Verywell Mind. www.verywellmind.com/how-do-you-live-in-the-present-5204439 (Accessed 12 March 2024).

Edmondson, A. (2023) *The Right Kind of Wrong: Why Learning to Fail Can Teach Us to Thrive*. London: Cornerstone Press.

Eikey, V. E., Caldeira, C. M., Figueiredo, M. C., Chen, Y., Borelli, J. L., Mazmanian, M. and Zheng, K (2021) Beyond Self-reflection: Introducing the Concept of Rumination in Personal Informatics. *Personal and Ubiquitous Computing*, 25: 601–616.

Fideler, D. (2014) *Restoring the Soul of the World: Our Living Bond with Nature's Intelligence*. Rochester, Vermont: Inner Traditions.

Forbes (2024) Forbes Billionaires List. www.forbes.com/billionaires/ (Accessed 12 May 2024).

Frankl, V. E. (2019) *Yes to Life: In Spite of Everything*. London: Ebury Publishing.

Gaither, S. E. and Sommers, S. R. (2013) Living with an Other-race Roommate Shapes Whites' Behavior in Subsequent Diverse Settings. *Journal of Experimental Social Psychology*, 49: 272–276.

Ganz, M. (2015) *Public Narrative in the Art of Change Making*. Atkinson, J., Loftus, E. & Jarvis, J. (eds). London: The Leadership Centre, pp. 174–176.

Gorman, A. (2022) The Big Question: Why Do We Tell Stories? *New York Times*. Guest Essay. www.nytimes.com/2022/12/08/special-series/the-big-question-why-do-we-tell-stories (Accessed 10 January 2024).

Grandmother Medicine Song (2023) Dreaming the 5th World Hopi Wisdom Teachings. https://hopiwisdomteachings.com/dreaming-the-5th-world-circling-community/ (Accessed 10 January 2024).

Greenberg, M. (2017) 8 Powerful Steps to Self-Love. *Psychology Today*. www.psychologytoday.com/us/blog/the-mindful-self-express/201706/8-powerful-steps-self-love (Accessed 12 December 2023).

Harrell, S. P. (2018) Being Human Together: Positive Relationships in the Context of Diversity, Culture and Collective Wellbeing. In Warren M. A. and Donaldson S. I. (eds) *Towards a Positive Psychology of Relationships*. Santa Barbara: Praeger.

Hawkins, P. and Turner, E. (2020) *Systemic Coaching: Delivering Value Beyond the Individual*. Abingdon: Routledge.

Inner Development Goals (n.d.) https://innerdevelopmentgoals.org/ (Accessed 10 December 2023).

Johnston, C. (2021) Today's Extreme Social and Political Polarization. *Psychology Today*. www.psychologytoday.com/us/blog/cultural-psychiatry/202107/today-s-extreme-social-and-political-polarization (Accessed 13 November 2023).

Kahneman, D. (2012) *Thinking, Fast and Slow*. London: Penguin.

Kashtan, M. (2014) *Reweaving the Human Fabric: Working Together to Create a Nonviolent Future*. Oakland, CA: Fearless Heart Publication.

Khilay, S. (2012) Playing the 'Race Card'. LSE Blog, Equality and Diversity. 2 May. https://blogs.lse.ac.uk/equityDiversityInclusion/2012/05/playing-the-race-card/ (Accessed 12 December 2023).

Kubin, E., Puryear, C., Schein, C. and Gray, K. (2021) Personal Experiences Bridge Moral and Political Divides Better Than Facts. *Proc Natl Acad Sci USA*. Feb 9;118(6): e2008389118. https://pubmed.ncbi.nlm.nih.gov/33495361/ (Accessed 10 January 2024).

Levine, P. (2010) *In an Unspoken Voice: How the Body Releases Trauma and Restores Goodness*. Vermont: North Atlantic Books.

Lucas, M. (2023) *Creating the Reflective Habit: A Practical Guide for Coaches, Mentors and Leaders*. Abingdon: Routledge.

Macy, J. and Brown, M. (2014) *Coming Back to Life*. Canada: New Society Publishers.

Mastini, R. (2017) Degrowth: The Case for a New Economic Paradigm. Open Democracy. www.opendemocracy.net/en/degrowth-case-for-constructing-new-economic-paradigm/ (Accessed 12 December 2023).

Menakem, R. (2017) *My Grandmother's Hands*. Las Vegas: Central Recovery Press.

Niemöller, M. (1945) When they came for me, there was no one left to speak up. Holocaust Memorial Day Trust. www.hmd.org.uk/wp-content/uploads/2018/06/First-They-Came-with-new-branding.pdf (Accessed 13 April 2023).

Pearce, L.H. (2016) *Burning Woman*. Shanagarry: Womancraft Publishing.

Ramamurthy, A. (2016) The Asian Youth Movements: Racism and Resistance. *Soundings*, 2016(63): 73–85.

Rosenberg, D. (2021) Remembering the Battle of Cable Street. https://tribunemag.co.uk/2021/10/remembering-the-battle-of-cable-street (Accessed 13 November 2023).

Rosenberg, M. B. (2015 [1999]) *Nonviolent Communication: A Language of Life*. 3rd Edition. Boulder, CO: Puddle Dancer Press.

Ryde, J. (2019) *White Privilege: Unmasked*. London: Jessica Kingsley Publishers.

Sanchez, A. L. (2017) *The Four Sacred Gifts: Indigenous Wisdom for Modern Times*. New York: Simon & Schuster Inc.

Scott, S. (2009) *Fierce Leadership: A Bold Alternative to the Worst "Best" Practices of Business Today*. Grangemouth: Praktus.

Scotton, N. (2023) Poem no 2, A Pocketful of Clouds. https://neilscotton.com/a-pocketful-of-clouds/ (Accessed 3 March 2023).

Shah, S. (2022) *Diversity, Inclusion and Belonging in Coaching: A Practical Guide*. London: Kogan Page.

Silvestri, K. (2023) The Power of Storytelling. *Psychology Today*. www.idrinstitute.org/wp-content/uploads/2019/02/DMIS-IDRI.pdf (Accessed 12 February 2024).

Soma Essentials (n.d.) Increasing Self-Awareness and Self-Compassion: A Guide to Somatic Healing. Soma Essentials https://somaessentials.com/increasing-self-awareness-and-self-compassion-a-guide-to-somatic-healing/ (Accessed 12 February 2024).

Standing Together (n.d.) www.standing-together.org/en (Accessed 12 February 2024).

Thomas-Olalde, O. and Velho, A. (2011) Othering and Its Effects: Exploring the Concept. www.academia.edu/42889355/Othering_and_its_effects_exploring_the_concept (Accessed 12 January 2024).

Tropp, L. R. and Godsil, R. D. (2014) Crossing Boundaries: How Intergroup Contact Can Reduce Racial Anxiety and Improve Race Relations. Psychology Benefits Society. https://psychologybenefits.org/2014/11/03/crossing-boundaries-how-intergroup-contact-can-reduce-racial-anxiety-and-improve-race-relations/ (Accessed 12 February 2024).

Underwood, J. E. (2020) Consensus Definition of Self-Love: A Delphi Study. Mercer University ProQuest Dissertations Publishing, 28154711.

UNICEF (2023) The State of the World's Children. www.unicef.org/reports/state-worlds-children-2023 (Accessed 12 March 2024).

Wheatley, M. J. (2024) *Restoring Sanity: Practices to Awaken Generosity, Creativity and Kindness*. Oakland, CA: Berrett-Koehler Publishers Inc.

World Economic Forum and McKinsey & Co. (2024) The Global Cooperation Barometer 2024. www3.weforum.org/docs/WEF_The_Global_Cooperation_Barometer_2024.pdf (Accessed 12 January 2024).

World Wildlife Fund (2022) Living Planet Report: Building a Nature-Positive Society. www.wwf.org.uk/our-reports/living-planet-report-20 (Accessed 10 January 2024).

4

Essays on Hope

And so I come to the penultimate part of the journey, where I invite others to give rich and varied perspectives, sharing their collective wisdom, and offering their insights into the subject of Othering.

The contributions are unique and varied in style, and come from across the globe. The women interviewed for this book were all resident in the United Kingdom. Here we open out to global friends and citizens, recognising our common human experience.

I begin with the wise words of Lily Seto, who invites us to simple but important actions and commitments.

Turning "Othering" into "Belonging"

Lily Seto

I am a Chinese Canadian woman, in my mid-sixties, born and raised in Western Canada. I respectfully acknowledge the W̱SÁNEĆ and Coast Salish Peoples whose traditional lands I live, work, and play on. I am married and am blessed with two sons and two grandchildren. I consider myself to be a successful global coach, mentor coach and coaching supervisor. And I acknowledge I use my definition of "successful". *What does this description of me conjure up for you, the reader?*

I own that I am in an incredibly good place in life and have many privileges. I have many opportunities to belong to diverse groups. This has not always been the case. This is my story of turning "Othering" into "belonging".

"Othering" is defined by the Cambridge online dictionary as "the *act* of *treating* someone as though they are not *part* of a *group* and are different in some way". Othering can be about attributes such as race, ethnicity, age, sexual orientation, country of birth or domicile, educational status, type of occupation or social-economic status. I was six years old when I first encountered the feeling of being Othered. I was starting elementary school and had moved to the Chinatown area of Vancouver from

DOI: 10.4324/9781003390602-5

a very small town where we were the only Chinese Canadian family. Interestingly, my Chinese classmates "Othered" me as a *banana*: white on the inside and yellow on the outside. And my white classmates did not consider me western enough to be their friend. It was a hard lesson on straddling two worlds. As I grew, I realised that I lived in a world where I needed to decide where I wanted to fit in and agreeing to things that may not feel right in order to belong. At times it meant compromising my values and identity for what the group demanded of me. It, as Toko-pa Turner describes, can split us in our loyalties (2017, p. 14). It may also invite us to second-guess ourselves and encourage us to remove ourselves from a situation or from joining a group, in advance of an anticipated rejection. This was all true for me. And, at some point, I rebelled against the unfairness of the system and worked twice as hard to fit in, by rejecting my Chinese roots, which is, as an immigrant family, our learned cultural way of fitting in.

When I was in my late thirties, I realised that I was exhausted from trying to fit in. It did not really work to reject my Chinese roots when the first thing people saw is what I looked like! There had to be a better way. I started to do my work on who I wanted to be in the world and set a loosely held plan to move towards bringing my authentic self to everything I do. When I discovered the concept of self-agency, I experienced my biggest shift. It meant that I could choose who I wanted to be in the world, how I lived my life and how I served the greater good. Some of my work embodied elements of Buddhism and spiritualism. And I also adopted the Indigenous perspective of becoming a good ancestor to past and future generations. This has been my guiding light to self-acceptance and coming home to myself. I have learned which groups are not worth belonging to and what groups I can create and invite Others into. I have also learned to look within before I look outside of myself. Coaching, and then coaching supervision, feels like a calling. My own ongoing development and supporting other coaches to do their work is very fulfilling.

I acknowledge that I can even catch myself "Othering". And I also accept that every encounter and experience has brought me to my privileged life, so I would not trade any of my experiences however hard it felt at the time. And, at the current time in my life journey, I am deliberately paying it forward, especially to those who may feel "Othered". For all those who have been and are a part of my journey, I honour and thank you for walking alongside me.

And, I invite you, the reader to consider:

1. being educated on the ideas of "Othering" and "belonging"
2. examine any of your biases (conscious or unconscious) that might surface
3. broaden your circle of colleagues and friends by inviting in people that you would not normally engage with, and
4. overcome the bystander effect by speaking up when you notice any "Othering" that may be happening.

Because true belonging only happens when we present our authentic, imperfect selves to the world, our sense of belonging can never be greater than our level of self-acceptance.

(Brené Brown, 2012)

References

Brown, B (2012) *Daring Greatly: How the Courage to Be Vulnerable Transforms the Way We Live, Love, Parent, and Lead*. London: Penguin.

Kishimi, I. and Koga, F. (2018) *The Courage to Be Disliked: How to Free Yourself, Change Your Life and Achieve Real Happiness*. Tokyo: Diamond, Inc.

Myss, C. (1996) *Anatomy of the Spirit: The Seven Stages of Power and Healing*. New York: Three Rivers Press.

Tipping, C. (2011) *Radical Self-Forgiveness: The Direct Path to True Self-Acceptance*. Boulder: Soundstrue.

Tolle, E. (2005) *A New Earth: Awakening to Your Life's Purpose*. Toronto: Penguin.

Turner, T. (2017) *Belonging: Remembering Ourselves Home*. Salt Spring Island: Her Own Room Press.

Now we hear from Andréa Watts, who uses creative approaches in her work as a coach. She also introduces us to the idea that just as we Other people we are in contact with, we use the same blinkers to Other self, potentially denying the richness of our intersectional identities.

Recreating the Narrative

Andréa Watts

I first came across the concept of "Othering" at the 2021 Hult Ashridge conference "Love over Fear". One of the keynote speakers delivered a powerful talk on the subject. Sharing a personal story, he illustrated how fear was the foundation of "Othering". His premise focused on the judgements we make. Whether consciously or unconsciously, these criticisms of others behaviour, values, culture and beliefs, and so on, come from a moral high ground. We elevate ourselves above those we judge, insinuating superiority by asserting, "I would not behave in that way!".

Rather than taking time to understand the other person, this attitude emphasises our differences as negative. This response is easier, serves the self-righteous ego and reinforces our individual and collective narratives about those being "Othered". The result of this closed thinking causes divisions between ethnicities, genders, sexual preferences, politics, religion and so on. Sadly, without self-awareness, everyone risks being both perpetrator and recipient of Othering.

The Distorted Narrative

Influenced by external narratives, I believe "Othering" is, unfortunately, something we also do to ourselves. We fail to be at peace with the breadth of our experiences, interests, preferences and character traits. Instead, we criticise and judge aspects of our personality, and in being at odds with the beautiful complexity of human nature, deny parts of our identity. It is noticeable that when not in this state of separation, we describe ourselves as holistic and authentic. I invite you to take a moment to reflect on this idea of "Othering" self.

Society has a pivotal role in this either/or approach to identity, seeking to limit and contain us in metaphorical boxes. But individuals are both a plumber and reiki healer, a database administrator and creative coach, a gamer and politician. These character traits are not mutually exclusive. Nonetheless, this fact remains at odds with the notion, created and perpetuated by external forces, that we can only be one type of person or another. This incorrect and distorted narrative influences how we view and treat ourselves and others.

By not understanding that different aspects of who we are can and do coexist, we project these limited versions of ourselves unto other individuals and groups. Determined to see them only in their boxes, we desire them to remain there because this is comfortable and does not challenge our version of reality.

Recreating the Narrative

Despite its roots in fear, how we relate to ourselves and society's metaphorical boxes, there are opportunities to negate "Othering". We can accomplish this by starting from a place of

love and lack of judgement. As we individually and collectively move away from the constraints of either/or ways of interaction towards the curiosity of inquisitive enquiry we can create more cohesive societies. While this can prove challenging, uncomfortable, unfamiliar and even potentially upsetting, it remains possible. Thankfully, there are creative tools that can help us connect with ourselves and others in a meaningful and accepting way.

Creating Connections Through Collage

Through the lens of imagery and the visual narratives possible in collage creation, the Collage Coaching Technique™ enables us to see connections made visible through our collage stories. Importantly, concerning "Othering", these connections occur on two levels, internally with self and externally with others.

With the former, shifts occur as the creative technique allows reconnection to a sense of identity and the wholeness that improves interaction with others. These shifts occur through the inherent qualities in collage creation of disassembling, disrupting, questioning, reassembling and visualising thoughts externally which simultaneously reconstructs internal narratives.

From a group perspective, the process facilitates relationship building as people create individual collages or collaborate to create a collective one. In both instances, the collage creator is the storyteller and in turn listener, so every voice has the space to be heard. While sharing, the storyteller feels seen as the listener remains fully engaged. There is a flow of rich and often emotional conversation emerging from the language of visual metaphors and symbols present in the collage. As people seek to understand the meaning held in the images, dialogue shifts from narrow either/or ways of expression towards inquisitive enquiry leading to more honest discussion.

Furthermore, deeper understanding and connections arise when the stories or images resonate with others. At these points, where stories overlap and journeys intersect, something powerful and beautiful happens. I have seen the surprise, joy and affinity when people share similar stories or attribute the same meaning to similar and even distinctly different images. At this moment, they see something of themselves in the other person and in doing so, feel connected. Therefore, rather than "Othering", the opposite is true. We recognise that individuals and communities who may superficially appear different to us, share more in common than what is different.

Hope Entwined in the Thread of Shared Emotions

I have witnessed thousands of collage creations and been privileged to hear countless personal stories. Because of this experience, I have learnt there is a thread that runs through every human story. Whoever we are, we experience emotional pain and pleasure in all its guises. While the triggers, intensity and response may differ, the emotions of anger, jealousy, loss, love, hope and courage, and so on, remain the same. This fundamental truth connects us on a most profound level.

By enabling us to experience this deep shared connection, the Collage Coaching Technique™ breaks down barriers and promotes acceptance of diversity. This shift allows us to stop feeling threatened by our differences and embrace their potential to complement and enhance, rather than diminish our sense of identity.

While I doubt we will completely eradicate "Othering", I remain hopeful that we can minimise it through deeper connections. As the conference title Love Over Fear suggests, let us engage with others from a place of love, seeking to bridge differences rather than stand in judgement from a place of fear.

Andréa's invitation to us is, therefore, to use our creativity and become more playful in our approach to fostering human connection. I have underlined the importance of storytelling and now I go to a poetically written piece jointly curated by a Christian Cathedral Dean and an Aboriginal leader from the Melbourne area of Australia. In 2023, a referendum to embed First Nations rights in the Constitutional fabric was unsuccessful and this contribution is gratefully received and I hope will serve to remind us of the enduring systemic inequality.

"yany-ndhu gulbara – So That You Understand"

Uncle Glenn Loughrey and Dean Andreas Loewe

ngadhu wiray [*not I*]

not I

who I am
is not mine
to declare

Others define
who what
I am

my story
is interpreted
mediated

through the
language of
the Other

the one
with the power
to designate

life
hope
possibility

or stereotypes
fitting
story

their meaning
making
myth

I am not I
I am who you
want to make me

since invasion
that is
how it is

nothing has changed
yany-ndhu gulbara [*so that you understand*]

Uncle Glenn Loughrey

The invasion of Aboriginal Country by British colonisers in the late eighteenth century ruptured a way of life and culture that had shaped the nation we now call Australia for more than 65,000 years. Settlers not only took Aboriginal land and killed its inhabitants, but radically changed a flourishing ecosystem by introducing European species and diseases.

People were forcibly removed from Country – the traditional clan lands where elders draw on their own deep cultural roots and ancient lore to nurture each successive generation – onto reserves and missions. That removal brought with it a loss of Aboriginal identity and voice. Quite literally: in missions the use of Aboriginal languages was forbidden, and the use of English enforced.

The effects of colonisation and removal from Country are still keenly felt by First Peoples today. Like a rock thrown into a lake, ripples continue to move out from the genocide of the 18th and 19th centuries to the lived experience of First Peoples in the second decade of the 21st. From the initial loss of Country, concentric "circles of loss" ripple out: loss of language, loss of kinship through the Stolen Generation – the forcible assimilation of Aboriginal People that could pass as white into adopted white families, loss of identity and, for many who have buckled under the colonial strain, loss of freedom and incarceration. The national story of First Peoples in Australia is still being told by the colonisers: for much of the 20th century our national history has predominantly been written by white people. Because the story of First Nations "is interpreted/ mediated/ through the language of/ the Other', through the 'meaning/ making/ myth' of the colonisers, Wiradjuri artist and Anglican priest Glenn Loughrey explains that 'I am not I/ I am who you/ want to make me".

While that perspective of Otherness continues to be true for countless Aboriginal People and Torres Strait Islanders today, Uncle Glenn's poem speaks into a particular setting and story: that of Jimmy Governor (born 1875, executed 1901). One of the last people to be declared an "outlaw" in the colony of New South Wales in mid-1900, Governor's life has been the subject of many famous retellings, including the Booker-prize listed fictional retelling of Governor's life by Thomas Kenneally (1978), and Les Murray's *The Ballad of Jimmy Governor* (1970). A household name for many Australians, Governor's story may be less known to readers elsewhere. Like Loughrey, Governor was a Wiradjuri man. Living in the Talbragar River region of New South Wales, Jimmy had courted teenage-settler Ethel Page with whom he had a son, and whom he married during her pregnancy. Because of their mixed marriage, the Governors were the object of much settler discrimination.

In his murder trial in late 1900, Governor recounted how his wife's employer, Mrs Mawbey, "said any white woman who married a blackfellow was not fit to live". The Mawbeys and their lodger, local school teacher Miss Helen Kerz, "were always poking fun at us and laughing. I was never a loafer ... I always worked and paid for what I got, and I reckon I am as good as any white man", the *Maitland Daily Mercury* reported Governor's defence (*Maitland Daily*, 1900). After a particularly egregious taunt by the teacher – "you black rubbish, you want shooting for marrying a white woman" as the *Mudgee Guardian and North-Western Representative* reported from the trial (*Mudgee Guardian*, 1900) – Jimmy "snapped under the colonial pressure of guilt", Loughrey tells. Jimmy Governor and his brother Joe killed the Mawbey family and the teacher.

During the next 14 weeks, the Governor brothers meted out revenge across north-central New South Wales, deliberately targeting any who had wronged him. Cunningly eluding colonial police and armed forces, Governor killed four more people in the process. After the first killing while on the run, Loughrey's own family story and that of the Governors intersect: Jimmy Governor "rode past the Loughrey house at Loughville and waved to those inside as he went to water his horses at the creek. In both cases – the Aulds and the Loughreys – did not know about the crimes he had committed, in the Loughreys case, the murder of Herb [Alexander] McKay a couple miles back toward the Gulgong Road". Governor would go on to kill again twice, in deliberately calculated revenge, to silence the voices of those who had taunted him. Loughrey comments:

> His "rampage" may have begun in an emotional outburst but the subsequent murders he committed were not. He had a long list of people who had wronged him, and he went methodically about the process of pay-back. These were people he knew, drank with, played cricket with, and worked for, cutting fenceposts among Other tasks. People he at one time or another saw as friends.

Almost three months after the murders of the Mawbeys and Miss Katz, Governor was dramatically arrested and moved to Sydney. The defence put forward by his legal counsel, Francis Boyce, that having been outlawed Governor could not be tried again for the crimes that led to the sentence of outlawry, was ruled out. He was hanged on 18 January 1901 at Darlinghurst Gaol. Loughrey reflects on the brutal end of story of retributive justice – to Governor and those whom he killed as pay-back for their racism:

> We do a disservice to him and many who have had to live with the colonial pressure of shame by simply pigeonholing him/them in a convenient category such as 'bushranger' and Other categories of deficit for our own purposes. It is much more complicated, and we owe it to them

to engage with the complexity in such a way that we respect the humanity of each, despite their actions.

In the same month in which Governor was executed, January 1901, the Australian Constitution came into force. In fact, Governor's execution was delayed so that it took place after the celebrations that marked the new Constitution. Although the Australian Constitution has been amended eight times by a successful national referendum since its inception, the foundational text of Australia still does not formally recognise First Peoples. "Since invasion/ that is/ how it is./ nothing has changed/ yany-ndhu gulbara [*so that you understand*]", Loughrey ends his poetic reflection on how Jimmy Governor's story in 1901 and the story of First Peoples in Australia in 2023 – including his own family story – continue to intersect.

One hundred and twenty-three years on, regarding and respecting the "humanity of each, despite their actions" continues to elude a justice system built on the retributive justice that led Governor to kill in revenge, and in turn killed Governor. Australia continues to incarcerate First Peoples in disproportional numbers to their white counterparts: while only 3.8 per cent of the Australian population identify as Aboriginal and Torres Strait Islanders, more than 32 per cent of inmates are from a First Peoples background (Australian Bureau of Statistics, 2023). "Proportionally, we are the most incarcerated people on the planet", Australian First Nations representatives observed: "We are not an innately criminal people. ... These dimensions of our crisis tell plainly the structural nature of our problem. This is *the torment of our powerlessness*", they concluded (Anderson et al., 2017, para 6–7). A new way of finding justice is urgently needed: one that is based on restorative, not retributive, justice.

That new way has begun to open up in the national movement set out in the *Statement from the Heart*. In 2017, 250 Aboriginal and Torres Strait Islanders were delegated by their home communities across Australia and the Torres Strait to come together as the First Nations National Constitutional Convention. They met at Uluru, at the great sacred red rock at the heart of the nation. While the *Statement from the Heart* does reflect on the ongoing effects of the symptoms of the "torment of our powerlessness" – such as the disproportionately high rates of incarceration of First Peoples, and the incredible rates of Aboriginal deaths in custody – it transcends any introspection. The *Statement from the Heart* is a movement of hope, a gracious invitation – in the theological sense of "grace" as a "sanctifying gift that is utterly undeserved".

The *Statement from the Heart* resolved to issue an invitation to white Australians, to walk alongside First Peoples "in a movement of the Australian people for a better future" (Anderson, 2017, para 12). The movement takes the form of a journey that first seeks to give First Peoples a place at the table by constitutional recognition; then a voice by enshrining a designated representative body advising Parliament and executive government on matters pertaining to First Peoples; before entering into the kinds of formal treaties that individual states have already advanced in Australia, and which Other Commonwealth Countries, such as Canada and New Zealand, have adopted many generations ago. At the end of this shared national journey stands Makarrata, a Yolŋu word for "coming together after a struggle". The architects of the *Statement from the Heart* explain:

> Makarrata is the culmination of our agenda: *the coming together after a struggle.* It captures our aspirations for a fair and truthful relationship with the people of Australia and a better future for our children based on justice and self-determination.
>
> (Anderson, 2017, para 10)

Makarrata will have an enduring effect on the nation. It is like "walking with limp after having been pierced in the hip by a spear", Uncle Glenn Loughrey comments. At the end of the journey, the nation that in its national anthem describes itself as "young and free" will have learnt that it is, in fact, ancient and tied to lore and customs from time immemorial. At the heart of that process stands truth telling. The realisation that the Aboriginal "story/ is interpreted/ mediated/ through the/ language of/ the Other". When the truth is told and owned, there can be space for the power dynamic to shift; the imbalance may begin to be righted. This is a restorative, not retributive justice. But the cost of this process will be just as high. It will be painful and traumatising for First Peoples to recall the stories of torment and powerlessness. It will be shameful and devastating for the descendants of colonisers to acknowledge the dispossession and genocide since first contact, and the ongoing ripples of discrimination and exclusion that continue to rip through our society. The impact of the "spear of Makarrata justice" that will "pierce the nation's hip" will be painful and lasting. It will change how we walk as a nation. Australia may well end up limping. But it is this walking-with-a-different-gait that will make it possible for First Peoples and Other comers to learn to walk no longer alone, side by side in different steps, but together.

"ngadhu wiray – not I", Loughrey called his poem. The shared journey to remove the barriers that discriminate and denigrate, to undo the very things that have power to turn the "I" into the "Other", is a movement of hope. The *Statement from the Heart* invites every Australian to join the "trek across this vast country" in search of justice (Anderson, 2017, para 12). All who live in this Great South Land are invited to join First Peoples and later comers in this "movement of the Australian people for a better future" (Anderson, 2017, para 12). Whether as a political party or interest group, a sports or life-saving club, or a church congregation such as ours at St Paul's Cathedral, Melbourne: all are invited to look back to the past and, out of the lessons learnt from the past, choose to shape a different, a fairer and fuller future for Australia. That movement is finally gaining momentum, with many different voices coming together to advocate and argue for the "substantive constitutional change and structural reform" that's needed to make First Nations' "ancient sovereignty shine through as a fuller expression of Australia's nationhood" (Anderson, 2017, para 5).

The Cathedral community has joined the journey, walking alongside First Nations leaders like Uncle Glenn Loughrey, whose artwork, poetry and story confronts us with the crimes of coloniality and encourages us to become a better, more complete, Commonwealth. At the end of that process may well stand a new "i" for Australia – a new national identity – and there may finally be justice for its ancient peoples. Makarrata will not be the justice that revenges and kills, destroys and incarcerates. But a justice that restores what has been broken and rebuilds what has been lost, and enables first and later Australians to move forward together into the future on new, shared pathways.

References

Anderson, P., Davis, M., Appleby, G., Brennan, S., Cama, B., Davis, A., Hunter, N., Larkin, D., Macgillivray, D., Scales, S., Scott, G. and Synott, E. (2017) The Uluru Statement from the Heart. The Uluru Statement.

Australian Bureau of Statistics (2023) Corrective Services Australia. "December Quarter 2022". March.

Kenneally, T. (1978) *The Chant of Jimmie Blacksmith*. Melbourne: Angus and Robertson.

"Trial of Jimmy Governor: Sentenced to Death". *Maitland Daily Mercury*. Saturday, 1 December 1900, 3.

"Trial of Jimmy Governor. Found Guilty, and Sentenced to Death". *Mudgee Guardian and North-Western Representative*. Monday, 26 November 1900, 2.

Murray, L. (1970) The Ballad of Jimmy Governor: H. M. Prison, Darlinghurst, 18 January 1901. *Poetry Australia* (35), 10–12.

The idea of shared pathways and moving together in a more positive way fills me with hope and joy.

We go back now to Canada and Janet Mrenica who has worked in partnership with Indigenous women following her own self work and period of discovery and awakening.

Hope, Truth and Reconciliation

Janet Mrenica

Greetings from the traditional, ancestral and unceded territory of the Anishinaabe and Algonquin Peoples, Ottawa, Ontario Canada. This greeting, a land acknowledgement, is a recent tradition in Canada, one that represents hope. Its truth and origins are held by the caretakers of Turtle Island, the Indigenous name for the landmass that Canada is situated on, and its increased usage is a societal response to Reconciliation with Indigenous Peoples.

This essay supports the expression of Hope as seen through my eyes, weaving systemic and relational lived experiences of Othering, micro-aggressions and blindspots; eyes that have also awakened to what I did not know and in turn, I have managed, studied and learned with curiosity about and with women who were born and lived in circumstances different than I, resulting in my commitment to be an ally and walk hand in hand with them in further discovery.

I am a white middle-class professional woman who has had access to and benefits from both the dominant system by birth and then through hard work, the system born from colonialism. In witness, I saw injustice around me and have raised gender and social issues for conversation and action all my life. Over the last 20 years I have realised the dangerous depth of inequality to which this culture practices dismissal and injustice to those other than white, resulting in various understandings and sensations of Belonging to the place where one lives. I also realised I had biases, blindspots and that in awakening, realised we all do have such.

Travelling outside Canada was where I felt like and was seen as one of many colours born into this world. Twenty years ago, a professional commitment brought me to Mississauga for one week and I experienced in my country for the first time what it was like to feel watched – the only white woman in a restaurant. As I dug into this new reality for me in the country I was born into, I became aware that it is not only the colour of skin that matters: the innate sense of empowerment that comes with it may be more important. The Canadian landscape has a changing population mix and the conversation by racialised women happening in Canada about what is needed for aligned empowerment is bringing me hope. Hope is seen in the voice of Annahid Dashtgard, a Canadian writer of Iranian origin who recently wrote:

> Mixed identity people will form the majority in North America, as well as increasing exponentially across the Globe. What will be lost if these future beings continue marginalizing their racial and cultural differences to act more white than the people around them, just as many women entering the workforce think that they can succeed only if they act more "male" than the men around them.

I am a history buff. Heros and Heroines, the explorers of the New Land, are the storytellers whose adventures I memorised at an early age. The voice of the story-tellers of this New Lands founding were primarily men. For the voice of women, I had to dig, dig deep into history for the rare voices. Margarite Bourgeoys associated with Montreal, now Saint, and who was an immigrant from France, was the first to make her presence known to me. Madeleine de Vercheres, born in the Quebec town of the same name, is a military heroine, having defended a fort. Kateri Tekakwitha, known as Lily of the Mohawks, an Algonquin-Mohawk Indigenous woman, who had many contacts with Jesuits in Kahnawake, south of Montreal, and was beatified, now a Saint. The hope I see is that today women, and women of colour, are writing and being supported to publish their lived experiences of the time they were living through loss of homeland, immigration, awareness of differences, living between two worlds, and creating a next generation here.

Canada as a country turned 156 years in 2023. Its history of cultural genocide to Indigenous People where the government supported specific policy directions to forcibly take Indigenous children from their families, convert those who survived the maltreatment of education systems and to assimilate them into Canadian society. This direction had the complicity of the missionaries of Christian churches as early as 1611.

Canadian society and the world are now aware of the significant intergenerational trauma that has resulted, of the thousands of unmarked graves of Indigenous children who did not survive the maltreatment of education systems known as Residential Schools. Learning about these schools, the policy framework and the commitment not to repeat such history is the hope seen in the Actions recommended by the Canadian Truth and Reconciliation Commission. There is now curiosity about and the application of Indigenous traditions.

Hope is seen in the training of facilitators in implementing Cultivating Safe Spaces, an Indigenous framework founded by Elaine Alec, who is a Sylix and Secwepmc woman and has roots with the Colville and Nez Perce nations. This framework has helped and is helping people struggling to understand what decolonialising and reconciliation looks like in practice. Individuals go from insecure and overwhelmed to being focused and empowered, so they are able to communicate and contribute effectively to transforming systems. Hope is seen in the uptake of training that promotes wellbeing, inclusion, validation and freedom in business, organisations, policies and procedures.

Hope is seen in walking in allyship with women who have lived experiences different than I. I am grateful for the opportunity to be paired with women of colour in leadership journeys and for the opportunity to be paired with women I would not normally see in my day: Thank you to Leadership Ottawa for this invitation to being in a new way and after 14 years strong bonds prevail – as an organisation you were ahead of your time! I see hope in conversations that lead to a door opening for women of colour to feel comfortable in leading conversations about micro-aggressions that they experience – rather than assuming white women are to lead them. I have supported and have witnessed the beauty of a colleague of colour in the social justice community, seeing her recognise and register her place in such spaces to facilitate and share her experiences in unravelling the stories of racialised trauma that underpin ''My Grandmothers Hands'' (author Resmaa Menakem). Such lived experiences in holding space to embody a new way, in my life, form the moments that are the ones I carry in my heart and soul, and that energise me. Hope is choosing mutual allyship. Hope is choosing lived experiences of white women walking with women of colour, for sharing, and co-developed spaces. I choose Hope.

Reference

Missions and Creations of Reductions (2015) *The Canadian Encyclopedia* Indigenous-French Relations | The Canadian Encyclopedia

Earlier, I briefly mentioned the power of the coaching profession to shift the dial. Now, we hear from Salma Shah who has invested significant energy in making the coaching profession more inclusive and focussed on creating belonging for all. She shares her perspective and offers a call to action for any coach practitioners and leaders in organisations.

Coaching for All: Building a Legacy of Belonging, Social Mobility and Equity

Salma Shah

My lived experience is one of social mobility which means my personal and professional circles today are diverse and enriching. With this privilege, I often find myself privy to jaw-dropping conversations which are insightful, intriguing and sometimes alarming. Yet, the more I listen, the more they are an affirmation that I am on the right track with my mission to raise the bar and make high-quality coaching accessible to for all.

I recall an instance where a group of parents whose children were privately educated were outraged that Oxbridge was prioritising state school children. Leaving the politics of the education system to one side, the language was very much "us" and "them", some even questioning whether children from lower socio-economic groups, despite getting into Oxbridge, had the capability to succeed in top-level careers such as medicine or law. I'm aware this is an anecdote and not everyone whose child is at a private school feels the same, but we also have to accept this is unlikely to be a one-off conversation.

A common theme in my work over many years is that if you are from a lower socio-economic group there is a high likelihood you have experienced subtle and explicit challenges or had to work extra hard to achieve the same results as your colleagues. Other challenges observed include isolation, exclusion, imposter syndrome, dysfunctional resilience and a lack of psychological safety; in some cases also being overlooked for promotion. These experiences inevitably have an effect, impacting talent retention and our deeper sense of belonging to our workplace.

It is important that we don't send out the message that individuals from lower socio-economic groups need fixing, instead that it is the "system" that needs to transform. However, there are strategies we can develop to thrive and build personal equity through building a deeper inner level of self-belief and confidence, being authentic and behaving skilfully, building our personal brand, investing in peer networks by helping others and networking externally and internally. Reaching out for coaching and owning personal development is critical.

Once an indicator that an organisation was inclusive, representative and fair, the term "diversity" is in danger of becoming a platitude, a token effort to tick a box. There is no denying that a mix of ethnic and cultural backgrounds and a variety of lived experiences is a strong step towards making your company more agile, more stable and more astute. But hiring diverse talent isn't enough. If an organisation doesn't leverage its diverse mix of employees – by understanding, supporting and inspiring – then the benefits are all but lost.

To deliver what is referred to as an *employee centric culture*, coaching is a critical tool in a successful organisation's resource profiles. It is a crucial asset in navigating the multi-layered complexities organisations are going to face in their new expanded role.

But how do you effectively coach, mentor or sponsor someone whose culture, sexual identity, family background, religious belief, social class or physical or neurological characteristics are very different from yours?

It's the workplace experience that shapes whether people remain and thrive or leave (or, worse, just survive). Boosting inclusion by enabling equity, promoting openness and fostering belonging is a key driver of a successful workplace culture. To make progress in these areas, organisations will typically require a step change in the level of courage and boldness they have displayed so far. They must also be ready to tackle sensitive topics around cultural norms, and to shine a spotlight on and apply consequences for individual behaviour, including that in management and leadership.

This is where coaching through a wider systemic lens of inclusion, belonging and equity becomes crucial to serving a diverse population. Training as a coach or being coached by someone who connects is akin to finding our north star. It can help you move forward with purpose, and it gives you a reference point to keep you moving in the right direction.

The beating heart of my work is grounded in the complex layers of our lived experience and our sense of identity. As the founder of Mastering Your Power Coach Training, an award-winning accredited coach training programme, I am proud that it is unique as the only accredited coach training program designed with a wider systemic lens of inclusion, belonging and equity as a golden thread. Diversity, equity, inclusion and belonging is not simply tagged on at the end of the programme.

Coaching goes farther and deeper than mentoring. We know from our work with clients that sustained personal development, inner-work and growth requires time and psychological safety, with regular input and opportunities for check-in.

We need to give diverse voices the platform to talk about why we need to see diversity in the coaching profession. These voices need to be respected and heard. I, therefore, offer a call to action for coaching in organisations:

Does your organisation have a mandate to retain and develop a diverse (lived experience) intersectional talent pool?

Are all your internal coaches capable of coaching through a wide lens of equity, belonging and inclusion?

Do you know how coaching is perceived by employees from under-represented minority groups?

Despite the challenges, I have hope that we are making a difference in this space. Many of our clients are committed to making a difference and others (forgive the pun) know they need to address this.

Reference

Shah, S. (2022) *Diversity, Inclusion and Belonging in Coaching*. London: Kogan Page.

We now move to South Africa and two perspectives on the complex issue of colour and language in a nation where despite being colloquially known as the "Rainbow Nation", tensions and divides exist.

First, I invite the wisdom of Jennie Tsekwa, an academic and coach from Johannesburg who works in the area of diversity, equity and inclusion. She offers us three "lessons", an invitation to act, sharing her own experience to give readers insight into the discrimination she sees because of the choices she has made.

Holding Hope with Open Hands

Jennie Tsekwa

When I was about eight years old, we had just moved to Malaysia from the United States, and I wished desperately that my skin was a few shades darker than it was. With our fair, easily sun-burned skin and light-brown hair, my family stuck out and I wished more than anything that I could just blend in with the other kids in our Chinese neighbourhood.

What I didn't realise at the time was what having light skin actually meant in that context. I didn't understand the shelves of skin-lightening lotion in the shops, or why the expat adults thought it was so funny when local people called after us: "*Orang putih, orang putih!*" (which means "white person, white person" in Malay).

I could feel in my gut that there was something more going on – something about insiders and outsiders, and colonised and coloniser, and superiority and inferiority – but I didn't have the words for it back then.

Yet even without the words, I started becoming acutely aware of "othering". It usually starts in one's family first – how you are different from your siblings or cousins. Taller, shorter. Smarter, not as smart. Outgoing, shy. And at first, there is nothing wrong with noticing differences. In fact, in terms of human development, we all need to go through the individuation phase to figure out what makes us unique and different, and what makes us similar and gives us a sense of group belonging.

However, it usually doesn't stop there. It becomes problematic when those differences and similarities quickly get solidified through labels, assumptions and power – who is allowed to be where and with who and doing what. We get trapped into boxes based on how others see us, regardless of whether this matches how we see ourselves. And it's even harder when judgements are made and meanings attached to things we are born with and have limited choice about, like the colour of our skin, the texture of our hair, our physical features or our sex or perceived gender.

And then another layer of damage is added. As a result of centuries of white supremacy, patriarchy, imperialism and many other oppressions, some traits are seen as *inherently* better than others, and then these traits are linked to each other. Like the lighter your skin is, the smarter you must be. Or the more "feminine" you are, the more attractive you are. Or if you come from a country with more economic power, you should be given more respect or a position of authority.

And yet for most kids, no one tells you that these things are socially constructed, so you start internalising them and believing them to be the ultimate truth about you or your "group" and about other people and their groups. This is why deconstructing our belief systems about difference and identity is so important. We need to unlearn all the spoken and unspoken messages that have informed how we see ourselves and see other people – particularly around the damaging categories of race and gender, among many others.

In my mid-20s, I was introduced to three core concepts that have fundamentally helped me in my un-learning and re-learning journey, and in finding hope in turbulent waters. The first was Critical Diversity Literacy. Also known as CDL, this programme or framework for social change was developed by Professor Melissa Steyn in South Africa, who was inspired by the idea of racial literacy, which was developed by critical race theorist France Winddance in the context of the United Kingdom, as well as other critical theorists that Steyn references in her work. It provides ten principles for becoming more literate or more aware of how power is operating across and within differences and the experience of *othering* or *being othered*.

Second, I was introduced to the idea of internalised inferiority and internalised superiority through the work of the late Margaret Legum, a gifted facilitator who helped me see that someone can be a "nice" person and yet still carry deeply embedded ideologies of racism, sexism and other -isms that need to be addressed. And linked closely to this, I was finally exposed to an *accurate* history of the construction of race and racism, and grew in the hope and realisation that if we have been so deeply programmed as humans, we can de-programme through intentional commitment to anti-racism.

In my late 20s, my marriage across racial lines brought these lessons home in a whole new way. Despite the ideals and hope for a better and more equitable world for everyone, violent othering is a still a daily experience for individuals and groups that have been historically and currently marginalised and disenfranchised. I saw my husband, who identifies as a black South African, experiencing racial slights that I had never seen before. A colleague of colour shared with me that the experience is like "death by a thousand cuts", micro-aggressions that are often hard to prove and so frequent that they can lead to diversity fatigue and transformation burn-out.

So where do we find hope in a world where othering is so pervasive?

People often ask me this question in my work as a diversity, equity and inclusion consultant, and I haven't always found it easy to answer. However, I started finding hope in an unexpected place …

… when our three boys started asking my husband and I really tough questions about race. In engaging with them, and confronting my own inner fears and questions, my hope was reignited. So, I'd like to briefly share three stories with three lessons in hope.

Lesson 1: Break the Categories

When one of our sons was about seven years old, I found him staring closely at his open hands and turning them back and forth, saying: "pink", "brown", "pink", "brown", as he was noticing the shade of skin on the top of his hand and the shade of skin on his palm. He didn't comment further, and I didn't say anything. But I noticed he seemed quite concerned. It happened again a few days later but this time his demeanour had completely changed. After again the "pink", "brown", "pink", "brown" – he exclaimed, "I'm both!" And I felt deeply hopeful and deeply challenged.

Often, we as adults are the ones who impose phrases like – "you're half black, half white", perhaps somehow thinking this will be helpful in navigating a mixed identity. But my son is not half anything. He is whole. There is a very painful kind of othering that happens for people who don't fit into the boxes that other people think they should fit into. So, one of the very practical and loving things that we all can do is to stop trying to figure out *what* people are, and focus on *who* they are instead, including being loving towards ourselves if we are one of those people who don't fit the categories.

Lesson 2: Share More with Our Kids Rather Than Less, and Share the Truth

On another occasion, I was fetching one of my other sons from aftercare at school on a Friday afternoon. As I approached the gate, I could see him chatting with a friend who I didn't recognise. In hushed tones, I overheard his friend ask with some credulity, "Is that your mom?" He was clearly confused by how different my son and I look from each other. I couldn't help but smile when my son whispered back, "Don't worry, we'll talk about it on Monday."

The whole encounter could have happily ended there. However, it then took a very strange turn. The teacher, who had also been standing by the gate and listening to the conversation, said to the friend, "You see, the reason why Lesedi looks different from his mom is that Lesedi's dad adopted Lesedi's mom and that's why their family doesn't look normal."

I could feel my sharp intake of breath and the blood rising inside me. Not only was she giving this child false information, a distorted view on adoption and judging our family as "not normal" but I could see by the child's face that he was even more confused than before. As I tried to take a few breaths to compose myself and find the right words to respond, my son was already a few steps ahead of me. Looking the teacher straight in the eyes, he said confidently, "No, that's not true. My mommy's DNA mixed with my daddy's DNA and the DNA of all our ancestors and THAT is why I am the way I am."

I didn't need to say anything more after that. The teacher clearly got the point. And I was proud of my son for standing up for himself. I was also surprised because I had no idea that he even knew what DNA was.

So here was another important lesson. Without even realising it, my husband and I had been building our son's confidence by talking about our roots, our complicated history and ancestries and he was able to draw on that knowledge when he needed it. Many parents and teachers have told me that they are worried that they will pass on baggage to their kids if they talk about such things, but the next generation needs us to share more with them rather than less. They need the truth, and they want the truth, and this gives me hope.

Lesson 3: Honour Differences and Similarities But Hold Them Lightly

I have a third memory of another powerful learning moment that happened when our twins were even younger than in the previous two stories. They were probably about four years old, and I remember the conversation clearly. We had just gotten home from pre-school. They were eating a snack and one said to the other pointing to his chest, "Did you know that boys have triangles and girls have hearts inside?"

I had to stop myself from laughing because it was funny and cute, but I could see by the look on his face that he really believed this was true. And I was suddenly struck by how young the conditioning starts. They don't have any sisters and not much interaction with girls outside of school and I realised that if I didn't process this with them it could easily lead to all kinds of conclusions – like the stereotypes that boys don't have feelings, boys don't cry, girls are too sensitive, and so on.

And so, I slowed down my inner dialogue and started talking with them about it. What made them think so? And before long, one of them looked at the other and said, "But boys and girls both have feelings so maybe we are not that different?"

It turned into a very interesting conversation (at a four-year-old level, of course!) about differences and similarities and how both are important.

There is an important lesson and question here. How do I catch myself when I cross the line from seeing another person as different, to seeing them as less than me, or less than human? Less deserving of care. Less deserving of respect. Less deserving of all the things that I might take for granted. And what do I do when I see myself or others see me as the one who is "less than"?

If we become too attached to our idea of ourselves, or our idea and perception of those we see as similar or different to ourselves, our hope for the future is built on very shaky ground. It will lead us to holding onto things, rather than holding our beliefs and ideas about each other with humility and open hands.

Concluding Thoughts

What is the link between these three lessons and building a world that is more equitable and inclusive? For me, they are a regular reminder that we truly do need to start by unpacking our own stories, our conditioning and our beliefs, by doing the deep work inside ourselves and with others. It also helps to remember that there are very practical things that we can do as we relate to our children and the young people in our lives. And as we teach them, they become our teachers.

Rather than imposing our own categories and paradigms onto the next generation, we need to allow them to ask questions about themselves and the world, to point out where we are getting it wrong and how we can do it better. And we need to constantly be aware of when differences are weaponised and when othering is violent, and actively stand with those who are marginalised and oppressed. This requires a new understanding of our place in the universe – as both tiny and mighty – in order to have the right perspective on self and on any other human being we meet. In the wise words of old, our calling is "to act justly, to love mercy and to walk humbly". This is where hope lives.

Another South African coach of white origin shares a very different experience in her exploration of race and shade in the Country. Colleen Qvist writes about her experience of feeling unheard and dismissed in a dialogue about colour, inviting the reader to think about who has a legitimate voice in this space. Anyone who knows Colleen knows she is a formidable woman and yet, here, she describes being silenced.

Red and Yellow, Black and White

Colleen Qvist

My first exposure to the fact that people exist in skins of different colour or hues was probably the chorus:

> Jesus loves the little children
> All the children of the world
> Red and yellow, black and white
> They are precious in his sight
> Jesus loves the children of the world.

As a South African, I understood the black and white part although I realised that technically my skin is not white. Even as I am writing this, I am staring at my forearms and seeing that they are a tanned brown although the parts of my body that do not see the sun are definitely closer to white. As a child, I did wonder about these red and yellow children though and in a socially unconnected world, I never did get to see red or yellow skin.

As I grew up in the 80s, the rage amongst white people was to be tanned and there was no such thing as to be "too tanned" or "too thin". Every year I would go to the beach for a four-week holiday with my parents and be sure to get a tan dark enough that it would last the entire year. Many of my friends would tan back at home, far away from the beach, and would use baby oil and lie baking on sheets of aluminium foil in their gardens. Anything to be darker.

Fast forward more years, I became aware of skin cancer in sun-exposed skin. Suddenly lying in the sun like a lizard became a rather silly idea. It is then that tanning beds became popular. The focus was on getting the tanned skin but without the cancer risk. Of course, now we know that tanning beds still have a risk of cancer. I also realised that as much as white people were trying to become darker, there were those who were trying to become lighter and chemically burning their skins in the process. It seems that there is great value in having a light skin except to those fair-skinned people trying to become darker. The skin-lightening and whitening industry is big business with profound negative impacts on wellbeing and adverse effects on the skin. I found this ironic.

As an adult, I am more aware that "skin tone" for underwear or pantyhose/stockings has thousands of meanings, as does trying to find the foundation that is an exact match for your skin. I totally understand that all those different tones need a name or number, or both, so that you know for the following time which product you should buy. This means that names like truffle, suede, ivory, mahogany, champagne and porcelain exist. These names seem above board to me because they refer to products. It is when we start calling people by these names that I start to feel uneasy. I have been reflecting on why I feel uneasy, and I think it could be because we have recently stopped identifying people by their traits. We no longer say "The depressed child" but the "child who is depressed". We are saying that depression does not define the child any more than tallness or shortness should.

One term in particular that is used by Black people is "yellowbone" to denote a very pale skin tone in an African person. I recently witnessed this term being used to describe someone and I reacted as I find the term disrespectful. I was assured that it is in simple terms a way to explain the lightness of skin of an individual and is not meant as disrespectful. I was also assured that it is not the colour term that is offensive but the tone of voice. This person went on to explain to me that Africans have other descriptors for darker hued people like dark dindi and chocolate. They also mentioned that it was colonisation that demonised blackness and raised whiteness as a preference. This is, then, where the conversation ended and I felt dismissed for not understanding their perspective and subsequently silenced.

Unfortunately, people do still place a higher value on certain hued skins and the terms are more than descriptors. My feeling is that using the same terms in different contexts muddies the waters and propagates that some skin tones have more value than others.

How then do we end the effects of colonisation that demonised blackness and raised whiteness as a preference if the very people that this affected defend themselves in using terms that allow for the differentiation of a person's value based on the shade of their skin?

This is so interesting, both in how power can shift and is not necessarily held by the white person, but also in how communities of colour have embedded practices and language that continue to reinforce colonial beliefs. We sometimes collude in internalising our oppression.

The focus of this book is primarily the lens of race, however, in broadening out our consideration of Othering, I now offer a different perspective which shows the negative impact of assumptions and the beauty and impact of a kind act. Jess Lazarczyk, a talented organisational development practitioner has another important role; the mother of a son with autism. Here she beautifully shares the positive impact of being seen with love, an inspiration to us all to practice those small acts of kindness. This also brings me back to the power of somatic; a single touch held such power.

Would You Like a Cup of Tea?

Jess Lazarczyk

I had looked forward to this trip for weeks: a day out with two of my friends and our gaggle of children. It was December and we were visiting a petting farm half-way between our houses.

Wanting to feed the children and get out of the freezing conditions, we ran straight to the café. After about an hour, having regained the feeling in our fingertips, changed the relevant nappies, and caught up on the Big Life Updates, we decided to head out onto the farm.

Transitions are always tricky for my pre-schooler. And, to be fair, when you're comfortably watching *Hey Duggee* next to a roaring fire with a bag of chocolate buttons, who *really* wants to enter into minus degree temperatures to look at a field full of sheep?

Knowing that it wasn't going to be as simple as saying "right, then, wellies on – let's go!", I encouraged my friends to go on ahead. It was more than a polite gesture on my part, it was a strategic move so that their presence wouldn't add extra pressure to my child, and – in truth – so they wouldn't witness if the transition descended into an autistic meltdown. They got it.

Mum knows best. Guess what happened? I had watched as my friends quickly and simply toggled the other children up in coats, scarves and hats, the little ones excitedly talking about which animal to go and see first, and whether they thought it was going to snow.

My child steadfastly stared at their iPad, and you could be fooled into thinking they hadn't even noticed the rest of our party had left. But I clocked a hunching of their shoulders, and an intensity to their finger-twitching movements, a self-stimulatory activity they often use to cope with change.

I quietly sat down on the bench beside them, talked about the animals outside and let them know that I was going to start getting them ready to leave the café.

Melt down.

An autistic meltdown isn't a temper tantrum. Autism is a neurodivergence involving not only the brain, but also the entire central nervous system. A meltdown feels like an attack on said nervous system. It is all-consuming, and deeply frightening for the person involved. It's also entirely involuntary and not something one can be coaxed, frightened or cajoled out of.

Forty-five minutes later, I was sat stroking my child's hair as they silently regained control, hiccupping from the intensity of their screams and cries. They were now at a stage where they could tolerate me touching them, occasionally peeking at me through the side of their eye to check I wasn't about to start trying to get them to move, again.

I'm a seasoned parent to a neuro-spicy child, I know what it's like for the simplest of things to turn into the most complex and emotionally draining scenarios. Whereas fellow parents might leave the house with bags packed with colouring pencils, dolls, trucks and books, my husband and I pack ours with ear defenders, pressure vests, sensory toys and a tablet loaded with my child's favourite programmes. I have trained myself to not take any notice of people staring, or hearing comments while I sit on the floor of a supermarket aisle, holding my child to keep them feeling safe when they're overwhelmed by a loud announcement.

But sat in this café, stroking my little one's hair, tears streamed down my face, a tough week at work and sleep deprivation resulted in a totally annihilated sense of emotional resilience.

In that moment I had never felt so awfully exposed while also feeling entirely invisible. It was a packed café. There were at least ten other families who were pointedly ignoring us and hissing at their children not to stare. I would occasionally clock anxious looks directed at us, whispered conversations and shakes of the head. I knew in that moment that the majority of that room had written my child off as either mad or bad – and me off as an incompetent parent.

The saying goes that it takes a village. On that day, it took just one other woman – a woman who worked at the farm and had popped into the café on her lunchbreak.

I felt a hand on my arm, and looked up to see a smiling face. Not the kind of smile I had bitterly grown accustomed to (a smile where the corners of a person's mouth actually manage turn *downwards*, often accompanied by a pitying furrow of the eyebrows). This smile was a light, bright, genuine smile that met her eyes. Quietly she said, in a beautifully matter of fact way, "Would you like a cup of tea?". The most innocuous of requests was the difference that made the difference that day. She didn't comment on my child, she didn't comment on my puffy tear-streaked face – she simply offered a lifeline of help. She simply **saw me**.

I often say that raising a child with autism isn't what's difficult. The difficulty is raising a neurodivergent child in a world built by neurotypical people, *for* neurotypical people. In a world which still sees the neurodiverse as *deficient*, rather than *different*.

My parenting experience is different to what I had expected it to be. It's different to the parenting journey that many of my friends, family members and colleagues experience. It's different, but it's not deficient.

I know that my child will experience exclusion and forms of discrimination throughout their lifetime. I know that I'm not always going to be there to protect them and keep them safe. This thought leaves me feeling like I'm drowning in despair.

And then I remember the smile of the woman from the café. The woman who wasn't too frightened to approach us. The woman who cared. The woman who saw us.

And I know there will be people out there who aren't frightened of my child. Who will care for them. Who will see them for all of their magnificence.

And I smile.

My last contribution comes from a client who I have seen grow in ways which are inspiring to watch. Despite suffering from racism at points in her life, she now has a comfortable life and yet she still invests considerable time and energy in mobilising for change in health care, championing the concept of compassion. Uma Krishnamoorthy is a consultant gynaecologist and deputy medical director working in the north west of England.

Compassionate Inclusion for Dignity in Belonging, as a Solution for "Othering"

Uma Krishnamoorthy

I am a 56-year-old, Indian born British woman, who is a gynaecologist, living in England, with my doctor husband. I am blessed with a loving daughter, who is a barrister, a caring son-in-law, who is English, and an adorable eight-month-old granddaughter. I recognise how privileged I am, in the contentment I feel with my family, career, and blessings of the rich, diverse experiences in my life. I also feel immense gratitude, for the challenges life graced me with, and helped shape me, to who I am today. A key part of this has been the "Othering experiences" that stretched my resilience, and continue to help me grow stronger.

I was born in the beautiful coastal state of Kerala, in South India, where I grew up, until I finished my schooling. I then moved, to the adjoining state of Tamil Nadu, which is my father's birthplace, to continue higher education in medical school. Moving between the two Indian States of Kerala (my mum's birthplace) and Tamil Nadu (dad's birthplace) as a child, and moving countries from India to England after marriage, were richly memorable experiences. My parents had a love marriage not arranged by families, which was rare for their generation in India as they belonged to different states, spoke different languages and were of different social classes, caste and culture, which was the backdrop to my "Othering" experiences early on.

"Othering" is a phenomenon in which some individuals or groups are defined and labelled as not fitting in within the norms of a social group. It is an effect that influences how people perceive and treat those who are viewed as being part of the in-group versus those who are seen as being part of the out-group. Othering can be thought of as an antonym of belonging. Where belonging implies acceptance and inclusion of all people, othering suggests intolerance and exclusion.

My earliest memory of experiencing "Othering", is when I was about eight years old, when my teacher introduced me to the class as "The New Tamil Girl" who joined us this year, as I had to move schools. Little did she realise the precedence she was setting, albeit unintentionally, for the whole class to continued calling me so.

Even my cousins on my maternal side called me "Paandikkaari", which translates as "The Tamil girl", which was often for fun, so they thought, but left me with a strange distressing feeling of excluded, and not belonging. I felt alienated, whenever they othered me, on account of my mixed Tamil Kerala heritage. I was mindful throughout childhood that my father was from a different background to them, being from a mediocre working-class family in addition to other differences, unlike my privileged, rich and educated maternal side family.

> Compassion is a sensitivity to the distress of self and others with a commitment to do something about it. It is one of the most important declarations of strength and courage known to humanity. Compassion gives us the courage and wisdom to descend into our suffering.

I see compassion and inclusion as two sides of the same coin. "Othering" causes distress from exclusion, while Compassion aims to alleviate that distress, through inclusive actions, which I experienced in abundance from many, beyond close relatives and friends. The irony was, when I moved to Tamil Nadu in later years, I was called "The Kerala girl". In later years, been called a "Paki" and sworn at by patients besides covert and insidious, othering experiences too, as an overseas doctor in England. What stands out for me when I look back is that one can learn to identify "othering", and develop strategies for tackling such experiences, through self-compassion, emotional intelligence, and resilience building in self, while trying to enable others to understand, from the recipient's perspective, although the latter is not always easy. I had learnt early on to intuitively be acutely aware of, and recognise those who "othered", consciously or unconsciously, and learnt it was a reflection on them rather than me, and this awareness is key.

Kaniyan Poonkundanar, the Tamil poet and philosopher, emphasises the universal connectedness of humans, in that we are all the same, and the same moral values and codes apply to all of us. The original poem roughly translates to *every village is my village and every person is from my kin.*

Treating all equally, through a compassionate, inclusive approach of common humanity, was well instilled by my parents, from early childhood, based on this code. The result of the above is an ability to appreciate the connectedness of common humanity of this universe, celebrate the uniqueness of everyone, with all their imperfections through embracing the concept of "Wabi-Sabi", which means "Perfection in Imperfection". They taught me how to treat all with utmost compassion, and inclusion, upholding their dignity, and respect, regardless of religion, colour, class, caste or creed. This was quite uncommon in India then, and to lesser degree even now, half a century later, in some parts, as readers may be aware.

My life has been bestowed with abundant love, kindness, care and support, from friends, family, colleagues and even strangers. At the same time, there have been on and off "othering" experiences, sometimes even from good, intelligent people, well known to me for many years, and who are generally kind and compassionate. My observation is, they behave differently, in what they perceive as their "in-groups", with "Othering", directed at who they perceive to be in "out-groups", which is well recognised in the medical world. Enabling compassionate, and inclusive actions, to make anyone we come across feel a sense of belonging, to uphold their dignity, is something I learnt and practiced from an early age because this teaching was part of my childhood.

> Our universal yearning for dignity drives our species and defines us as human beings. It's our highest common denominator, yet we know so little about it. It's hard for people to articulate exactly what it is. Dignity is not the same as respect. Dignity is an attribute that we are born with – it is our inherent value and self-worth. Respect is different. Although everyone has dignity, not everyone deserves respect. Respect must be earned. Dignity is something we all deserve no matter what we do. It is the starting point for the way we treat one another. It is imperative to respect each other's dignity
>
> (Kaniyan Poonkundanar, 192)

I hope you, as the reader, on reading my brief offering, feel motivated to always practice Compassionate Inclusion mindfully, for enabling Dignity in Belonging for all, as this could be our solution for "Othering". It is incumbent upon us to infuse these values in our children, grandchildren and the younger generation, as well as among all the leaders in our organisations and systems. With mindful practice of compassionate inclusion, we can certainly hope that the universal connectedness, and love of common humanity, that transcends all differences without "Othering", that the 6th-century BCE poet wrote about, can become a current lived reality for all, and make this world a better place.

References

Cherry, K. and Mattiuzzi, P. (2010) *The Everything Psychology Book: Explore the Human Psyche and Understand Why We Do the Things We Do*. New York: Adams Media Corporation.

Gilbert, P. A. (2009) *The Compassionate Mind*. London: Little, Brown Publishing Group.

Hart, G. L. and Heifetz, H. (1999) *The Four Hundred Songs of War and Wisdom: An Anthology of Poems from Classical Tamil: The Puṟanāṉūṟu*. New York: Columbia University Press.

General Medical Council (2019) Fair to refer: Reducing disproportionality in fitness to practice concerns reported to the GMC. www.gmc-uk.org/-/media/documents/fair-to-refer-report_pdf-79011677.pdf General Medical Council, Accessed 15 December 2023.

Hicks, D. (2018) *Leading with Dignity: How to Create a Culture that Brings Out the Best in People*. London: Yale University Press.

Poonkundanar, K. (192), translated by G. U. Pope 1906, https://master04132.wordpress.com/2015/03/01/kaniyan-pungundranar-yaadhum-oore-yaavarum-kelir/ (accessed 15 November 2023).

I thank all the contributors to Essays on Hope. A book about human connection would have felt strange told in a single voice, and the fact the contributions span such a wide geography but have so much commonality heartens me in terms of demonstrating the existence of a connected and global movement.

There are many more voices. Join us in this song!

5

The End of This Journey

I come back to the women in this book and the courage they have shown in overcoming systemic disadvantage. Their stories have been an inspiration to me and left me absolutely convinced of the need for more female energy if we are to navigate the coming decades in a positive way. The past has also inevitably shaped our current reality. The book has offered some insight into why we form in-groups and out-groups, and how this leads to systemic inequality and the occurrence of Othering. It is not intended to provoke guilt or despair, but to build a basic understanding which can then form a foundation for us to move collectively into active hope and individual and community action. I offer some thoughts in terms of how this activism may emerge. There will be many others. My plea to the reader is: do not disengage and figuratively put your heads in the sand. I strongly suggest that the current political and social landscape and modes of governance will not enable us to find solutions and mitigations for our current challenges. We can all influence how our communities develop and evolve.

I am curious as to where you, the reader, now are. I hope you have made it to the end of this book. I know some of the content is complex and deep, and I also accept that you may not agree with parts of my worldview. If this book has, however, impacted you in any way or triggered some curiosity, I offer you the following reflective activities:

For Everyone

Invitation 1: Know Yourself

For a week, spend some time beforehand reflecting on what assumptions you are taking into each and every conversation; either at work or with family and friends.

DOI: 10.4324/9781003390602-6

Invitation 2: Notice Your System

Spend some time noticing the hidden cultures in the organisations you are in or engage with. Where is the power? Are there systems in place that promote exclusion?

Invitation 3: Connect with Nature

Take a mindful moment in nature every day. Close your eyes and listen to bird song; watch the sway of a tree; anything that connects you to the planet.

Invitation 4: Get Curious About Difference

If you don't already, intentionally get to know someone from each of the main world religions. If you know people already, have a conversation about their culture and norms specifically.

Invitation 5: Be More Activist

Think about what you might want to do to apply pressure to political systems to create positive rather than divisive narratives. What might you commit to change in your organisation?

Invitation 6: Slow Down

This might seem contrary to much of the previous suggestions, but slow down. Learn to be in the moment, connect with your body and learn to accept that as an individual you are simultaneously important and inconsequential.

For Coaches and Practitioners

Invitation 7: Informed Practitioner

Reflect on whether you know enough about systemic inequity and the impact of racial trauma. If not, educate yourself.

Invitation 8: Impact for Good

Reflect on who you are working with and giving your energy to. Is your work reducing or increasing inequality? Be honest!

Invitation 9: Offering Hope and Agency

Could you do more to raise awareness about the interconnectedness of our challenges and to paint a positive path in terms of the choices we can individually and collectively make?

Join us in whatever way feels right for you on the continued journey. Hold the hope close to you, and hold the despair at bay. Remember what the best of humanity can be.

And being human includes the power of creativity, and so I end this book with a short poem I have been inspired to compose, which I offer to you in hope.

> We build walls: real and metaphorical
> We buy into the scarcity mindset
> And the need for growth
> For more things, for more choice
> And with that choice, we lose fragments of our souls
> Of our humanity
>
> We mutilate and plunder
> Plunder from others who we deem less human
> Plunder from the Earth, which cannot satiate our greed
> And the rich get richer
> Whilst seeking further planets to commoditise
> For they believe in their invincibility
>
> Where are the warriors who dare to imagine?
> How can we rediscover what it is to be human?
> Can we create communities that truly value difference?
> And what might that difference coming together enable?
> Can we believe in abundance; in sufficiency?
> Can the best of humanity be rekindled in sacred flame?
>
> Let us believe in active hope
> In possibilities unimagined
> Let us step into the unknown work, individually and collectively
> And through this, let us find peace and calm
> Let us find wholeness
> **And may we then live together wholeheartedly.**

Glossary of Terms

Some key concepts such as the definition of othering are given in the text. I am conscious not all readers may be familiar with the terminology presented in this book. I, therefore, offer the following as my understanding of some of the less universally known language used. This is not a definitive truth, and I am conscious definitions can be a cause of dispute and debate, however, this is my interpretation of the concepts to aid the reader in their understanding.

Global North This is linked to geography as most of the Global North is in the Northern Hemisphere, however, it relates to socio-economic factors and poverty. Most of the Global North has high standards of living, whereas the Global South is more characterised by poverty, poor health and housing and inadequate infrastructure.

intersectionality The intersection, layering and overlap of multiple forms of identity which lead to discrimination; based on factors such as colour, gender, sexual preferences and class.

minoritised Individuals or groups who are discriminated against and disadvantaged because they are not part of the dominant group.

ally An ally is someone who is not from a minoritised group, but wants to understand their experience and take action to address inequality and the underlying causes of discrimination.

neo-liberalism Social and political policies which promote economic growth and free markets as the vehicle for advancement, normally attempting to enhance control by business while limiting government control and spending.

epistemological The theory of knowledge and how we construct what we believe to be true.

epigenetics Epigenetics is the study of inherited traits, or a stable change of cell function, that happen without changes to the genetic make-up of the cell.

ego-centric Thinking only of oneself and not considering impact on other people, living beings or the wider system

eco-centric/anthropocentric Considering the Earth as the centre and viewing all nature as having inherent worth.

weathering An effect where physical and mental health is negatively impacted through prolonged exposure to political and economic marginalisation and racism.

imposter syndrome Feelings of self-doubt or feeling that one is going to be exposed as unable to perform in work or life in general. This is rarely backed up by evidence, but is linked to negative self-talk.

Index

Note: Page locators in **bold** refer to tables and page locators in *italic* refer to figures.

Printed in the United States
by Baker & Taylor Publisher Services